PROVISION
PROMISES

JOSEPH PRINCE

CHARISMA
HOUSE

PROVISION PROMISES by Joseph Prince
Published by Charisma House
Charisma Media/Charisma House Book Group
600 Rinehart Road, Lake Mary, Florida 32746

Visit the author's website at www.josephprince.com.

International Standard Book Number: PPTBN

Published in association with: Joseph Prince Teaching Resources
www.josephprince.com

21 22 23 24 25 ∿ 9 8 7 6 5 4 3 2 1
Printed in the United States of America

Contents

The thief comes only in order to steal and kill and destroy. I came that they may have and enjoy life, and have it in abundance (to the full, till it overflows).

—JOHN 10:10, AMPC

Introduction

God wants you to have an abundant life. That's why He gave you Jesus. And with Jesus comes every good gift.

My friend, through Jesus' finished work at Calvary, God has supplied every provision you need for every area of your life. Today, you have full access to His favor, wisdom, righteousness, abundance and peace.

Beloved, I pray that as you read and meditate on the provision promises in this book, you'll experience afresh the Lord's love, His abounding unmerited favor and His practical wisdom. I believe that as you do, you'll walk more and more in the abundant life that Jesus came to give you as promised in John 10:10!

Grace always,

Joseph Prince

CHAPTER 1

Your Provision Is Wrapped Up In Jesus

*Therefore do not worry, saying, "What shall we eat?"
or "What shall we drink?" or "What shall we wear?"
For after all these things the Gentiles seek. For your
heavenly Father knows that you need all these things.*

—**MATTHEW 6:31–32**

*Give all your worries and cares to God, for
He cares about you.*

—**1 PETER 5:7**, NLT

Your Heavenly Father Cares About You

Do not worry. Three simple words, mentioned *three* times by our Lord Jesus as He taught on not worrying about the necessities of life. Jesus really doesn't want us to worry about our needs!

"Pastor Prince, how can I *not* worry about my needs?"

My friend, it's because the Lord Himself assures you that "your heavenly Father **knows** that you need all these things", and **He wants** to provide them!

So if you are facing a pressing need today, or seeing lack in a certain area, take heart. Don't be discouraged. Your heavenly Father knows all about it and He is more than willing to meet that need because He loves you.

Beloved, you have a *good* Father who cares deeply about you and wants to provide for your every need. So don't worry. Cast every care to Him now and be at rest, knowing that He will abundantly provide!

...what man is there among you who, if his son asks for bread, will give him a stone? Or if he asks for a fish, will he give him a serpent? If you then, being evil, know how to give good gifts to your children, how much more will your Father who is in heaven give good things to those who ask Him!

—MATTHEW 7:9–11

Therefore I say to you, whatever things you ask when you pray, believe that you receive them, and you will have them.

—MARK 11:24

God Is A Good Father

How do we know that God is a good God and a good Father?

Jesus dealt with this question simply by asking another question: "If earthly fathers, imperfect as they are, know how to give good gifts to their children, don't you think that your loving Father who is in heaven will be even better?"

My friend, if your child asks you for bread, would you give him a stone? Certainly not. You would give him the best bread you can find. How much more then, will your heavenly Father give good things to you when you ask Him!

Beloved, know in your heart that God is a **good Father** to you. So if you need something today, just ask Him for it. And as you ask Him, believe that you *have* received it from Him, and you *will* have it!

You are
not alone
in this world.

You have a good *heavenly Father who* cares deeply *about you.*

For God so loved the world that He gave His only begotten Son, that whoever believes in Him should not perish but have everlasting life.

—**JOHN 3:16**

Then Abraham lifted his eyes and looked, and there behind him was a ram caught in a thicket by its horns. So Abraham went and took the ram, and offered it up for a burnt offering instead of his son.

—**GENESIS 22:13**

He who did not spare His own Son, but delivered Him up for us all, how shall He not with Him also freely give us all things?

—**ROMANS 8:32**

God So Loved You He Gave You Jesus

God is a good God. He is a God of **love**. But we will never know how much God loves us until we know how much He loves **Jesus**, because He gave us Jesus, His beloved Son.

Do you remember the story of Abraham in Genesis 22? Abraham's heart must have been broken when he led his one and only promised son, Isaac, up Mount Moriah to be sacrificed. But in the end, Isaac did not have to die because God provided a substitute—a ram.

The ram caught in the thicket was really a picture of Jesus, who would one day be arrested, and led up Mount Calvary to be crucified in our place for our sins.

My friend, God so loved His Son, but He so loved *you* too, that He was willing to give up His Son for you. That's how much He loves you! And if God was willing to give you heaven's best—Jesus—do you think that He will withhold anything good from you?

*But of Him you are in Christ Jesus, who became
for us wisdom from God—and righteousness and
sanctification and redemption.*

—1 CORINTHIANS 1:30

*…Christ, in whom are hidden all the treasures of
wisdom and knowledge.*

—COLOSSIANS 2:2–3

*…you are complete in Him, who is the head of
all principality and power.*

—COLOSSIANS 2:10

You Have Jesus—You Have Everything!

When you love someone deeply, you would want to give that person your very best. To show your love to that person, you would give him or her what you value the most.

My friend, that's exactly what God did when He gave you JESUS. Jesus is the apple of God's eye, heaven's darling Son. Yet, God gave Him up for *you* because that's how much He loves you. God wants you to have His very best!

And Jesus is God's best for us because when we have Jesus, we have EVERYTHING! Jesus is our wisdom, our righteousness, our sanctification, our redemption, our success. In Him are hidden *all* the treasures of wisdom and knowledge!

Beloved, you are truly rich because you have Christ. And in Christ you are COMPLETE. Don't wait to have this or that before you feel complete. You are *already* complete in Christ—your all in all!

JESUS CHRIST...

Wisdom From Above

Wonderful *Counselor*

Light Of The World

The Lord Our *Righteousness*

Kinsman *Redeemer*

Tower Of *Refuge*

The *Resurrection* And The *Life*

Prince Of *Peace*

The Lord Our *Provider*

Author And *Finisher* Of Our Faith

The Great *Physician*

Bread Of Life

Good *Shepherd*

Alpha And *Omega*

The *Way*, The *Truth* And The *Life*

Great *High Priest*

Great *I Am*

...OUR ALL IN ALL

Jesus—Your All In All, The Great I Am

When God gave us Jesus, He gave us everything. We are truly rich because we have Christ, our **all in all**.

My friend, when you need wisdom, Christ is your wisdom. When you need righteousness, Christ is your righteousness. When you need sanctification and redemption, Christ is both to you. When you need faith, He is your faith.

When you are fearful of the odds against you, He is your favor. When you are weak, He is your strength. When you are troubled and anxious, He is your peace. When you feel vulnerable, He is your shield. When you are lonely, He is your faithful companion. And when you are sick, He is your healing and health.

Beloved, Jesus is the great I AM and He says to you, "I AM to you *whatever* you need Me to be!"

Oh, taste and see that the Lord is good; blessed is the man who trusts in Him!
—PSALM 34:8

...the Lord your God turned the curse into a blessing for you, because the Lord your God loves you.
—DEUTERONOMY 23:5

By this we know love, because He laid down His life for us...
—1 JOHN 3:16

Behold what manner of love the Father has bestowed on us, that we should be called children of God...
—1 JOHN 3:1

See God's Love And See Your Provision

When you change the way you see yourself and God, you will see changes in your negative circumstances.

A lady from Tennessee discovered this when she was about to give up on her failing graphic design business. Around that time, she was given my book, *Destined To Reign*, which completely changed the way she saw herself and her career.

She said, "My mindset about myself, and more importantly, **how much God loves me** through Jesus Christ, began to change. I began to believe and see that *Jesus* is my success, that it's not my career that makes me a success...Within two months, I began to see my business turn around. Six months down the road, business is booming—I am receiving royalties each month that I never dreamed I would get!"

Beloved, believe that you *are* greatly, immeasurably loved by your Father in heaven, and you can't help but see His goodness in your life!

*Wisdom is the principal thing; therefore get
wisdom. And in all your getting,
get understanding.*
—PROVERBS 4:7

*Length of days is in her [wisdom's] right hand,
in her left hand riches and honor.*
—PROVERBS 3:16

*If any of you lacks wisdom, let him ask of God,
who gives to all liberally and without reproach,
and it will be given to him.*
—JAMES 1:5

*But of Him you are in Christ Jesus, who
became for us wisdom from God...*
—1 CORINTHIANS 1:30

You Have Jesus As Your Wisdom

God wants us to go after wisdom. Wisdom is the "principal thing", He tells us. We are not to go after riches. But when we have wisdom, all the things we seek will follow after us, including honor and length of days. So *never* make riches your goal!

My friend, if you lack wisdom, simply ask God for it. He will give it to you "liberally and without reproach". The truth is that He has already given you wisdom when He gave you Jesus, "who became for us wisdom from God".

So if you are facing a challenge at work and you don't know how to resolve it, say, "Jesus, You are my wisdom. I thank You that You will provide me with the best solution." If you have a wayward child, say, "Jesus, thank You for wisdom in loving and raising this child well."

Beloved, you are most blessed to have Jesus, in whom resides all the treasures of wisdom and knowledge!

For if by the one man's offense death reigned through the one, much more those who receive abundance of grace and of the gift of righteousness will reign in life through the One, Jesus Christ.

—ROMANS 5:17

But by His doing you are in Christ Jesus, who became to us wisdom from God, and righteousness and sanctification, and redemption.

—1 CORINTHIANS 1:30, NASB

All praise to God, the Father of our Lord Jesus Christ, who has blessed us with every spiritual blessing in the heavenly realms because we are united with Christ.

—EPHESIANS 1:3, NLT

Righteousness Is A Gift

You cannot merit God's blessings through your good works. All His blessings, including the blessings of provision, are wrapped up in the person of **Jesus**! When you have Jesus, you have the gift of righteousness and the abundance of grace completely by His unmerited favor. You cannot earn them, work for them or deserve them. They are gifts!

Jesus is your righteousness, holiness and redemption. You are righteous, holy and redeemed (and blessed) not because of your good works, but because you have received God's provision of His Son.

And because Jesus can *never* fail or be removed from the throne, you will *always* have Him as your righteousness, holiness and redemption! Now, put your hand on your heart and say this: "Jesus, because I have You, I will always be righteous by Your precious blood. All the blessings, provision and favor that belong to the righteous are mine today and I receive them by faith! Amen and Amen!"

to the praise of the glory of His grace,
by which He made us accepted
in the Beloved.
—EPHESIANS 1:6

For You, O Lord, will bless the righteous;
with favor You will surround him
as with a shield.
—PSALM 5:12

Love never fails...
—1 CORINTHIANS 13:8

You Are Highly Favored Because Of Jesus!

The Bible tells us that God has made us "accepted in the Beloved". The Beloved here refers to Jesus and the word "accepted" means "given special honor" or "highly favored".

My friend, because you have Jesus who is God's Beloved, and you are found in Him, you are also God's beloved son or daughter, *deeply loved* and *highly favored* by Him!

Now, because you are highly favored by God in the Beloved, you can expect to have favor with your spouse, children, colleagues, clients and yes, even your in-laws! When you speak, people listen. When you step into a room, it lights up. Everything you touch is blessed and increased.

Beloved, as the apple of God's eye, expect good things to happen to you each day. Expect divine protection because His favor surrounds you like a shield. Expect every need to be met by the One who highly favors you. Expect good, because you are precious in His eyes!

And when she rose up to glean, Boaz commanded his young men, saying, "Let her glean even among the sheaves, and do not reproach her. Also let grain from the bundles fall purposely for her; leave it that she may glean, and do not rebuke her."

—**RUTH 2:15–16**

The Lord will command the blessing on you in your storehouses and in all to which you set your hand, and He will bless you in the land which the Lord your God is giving you.

—**DEUTERONOMY 28:8**

Step Out By Faith Into Your Field Of Provision

She saw plenty of grain in the fields and she picked it all up. It was the much-needed provision for herself and her mother-in-law. What Ruth didn't know was that the owner of the field, Boaz, had actually commanded his men to "let grain from the bundles fall **purposely** for her", because she had found favor in his eyes.

My friend, isn't it cool when Jesus, our heavenly Boaz, **purposely commands** the blessings on us, and tells His angels to drop them along our way? All we have to do is to go out into the fields and "pick them up".

Beloved, because you have found favor in His eyes, the Lord is *purposely* dropping His blessings along your path every single day! Like Ruth, all you have to do is to step out into your field of provision. With eyes of faith, see doors of opportunities opening before you. Have the courage to apply for that job you have always dreamed about. Prepare and equip yourself, and go forth and pick up those blessings our Lord has already laid before you. Your future is bright!

For **God**
so loved you,
He gave you His best,
JESUS.

Because you have

JESUS,

you have

EVERYTHING!

Therefore, having been justified by faith, we
have peace with God through our
Lord Jesus Christ.

—ROMANS 5:1

For He Himself is our peace, who has made
both one, and has broken down the
middle wall of separation.

—EPHESIANS 2:14

What then shall we say to these things? If God
is for us, who can be against us?

—ROMANS 8:31

Who Can Be Against You?

My friend, today do you believe that God is for you and not against you? You see, the greatest blessing anyone can have is **peace with God** through Jesus Christ. To know beyond the shadow of any doubt that all your sins are forgiven is the greatest provision made for you on Calvary's hill.

Jesus took upon Himself all your sins at the cross. He absorbed all of God's fiery indignation and judgment against all your sins, past, present and future, so that you can be totally forgiven and have everlasting peace with God.

So today, there is nothing between you and God. There is no more sin, no more shame and no more condemnation! And if God is for you, who can be against you? Now, what will you do today knowing that all His favor, wisdom, heavenly provision and blessings are backing you up, and that you cannot fail?

Now may the Lord of peace Himself give you peace always in every way. The Lord be with you all.
—**2 THESSALONIANS 3:16**

Peace I leave with you, My peace I give to you; not as the world gives do I give to you. Let not your heart be troubled, neither let it be afraid.

—**JOHN 14:27**

Be anxious for nothing, but in everything by prayer and supplication, with thanksgiving, let your requests be made known to God; and the peace of God, which surpasses all understanding, will guard your hearts and minds through Christ Jesus.

—**PHILIPPIANS 4:6–7**

Jesus—The Prince Of Peace

No matter what challenge, crisis or circumstance you are faced with today, allow His provision of peace to flow in and through you. Jesus is the Prince of Peace. He came to bring you peace, to anchor and to establish your heart even through the most turbulent of times.

No matter how boisterous the storm appears, how high the unemployment rates are or how low the world economy crashes, allow His peace to reign supreme in your heart and mind. It's a peace that surpasses all human understanding, and it provides you safety, soundness of mind, stability and even sweet sleep.

How can you let your heart not be troubled nor afraid? By receiving a fresh dose of perfect peace directly from the Prince of Peace today. Turn your cares into prayers. His robust peace will bring you safely through every storm!

Beloved, I wish above all things that thou mayest prosper and be in health, even as thy soul prospereth.

—3 JOHN 1:2, KJV

…let them say continually, "Let the Lord be magnified, who has pleasure in the prosperity of His servant."

—PSALM 35:27

Do not fear, little flock, for it is your Father's good pleasure to give you the kingdom.

—LUKE 12:32

The Lord's Heart Is To See You Blessed

When John, the apostle of love, wrote the Book of 3 John, he was already an elderly man, who had walked with the Lord for many years. If any man knew what the Lord's heart for His people was, it was John.

John knew beyond the shadow of a doubt that the Lord's heart for His people is that they be blessed and be in health, even as their souls are blessed. It simply delights His heart when His people are experiencing blessings in **every area** of their lives.

Beloved, the Lord is *pleased* when you are happy and healthy, enjoying your marriage, children and career. He is pleased when you can put food on the table, and have more than enough to be a blessing to the people around you.

For if by the one man's offense death reigned through
the one, much more those who receive abundance of
grace and of the gift of righteousness will reign
in life through the One, Jesus Christ.

—ROMANS 5:17

...as sin reigned in death, even so grace might reign
through righteousness to eternal life through
Jesus Christ our Lord.

—ROMANS 5:21

The thief does not come except to steal, and to kill,
and to destroy. I have come that they may have life,
and that they may have it more abundantly.

—JOHN 10:10

So faith comes from hearing, and hearing
by the word of Christ.

—ROMANS 10:17, NASB

Jesus Wants You To Reign In Life!

I am sure you know that Romans 5:17 is a verse I love to preach on. It tells us that those who receive the abundance of grace and the gift of righteousness will **reign in life** through Jesus Christ!

My friend, when you reign in life, you reign over sin and destructive addictions. You reign over sickness and disease. You reign over poverty and lack. In other words, you reign over anything that holds you back from experiencing the *abundant life* that Jesus died to give you!

Beloved, the Lord's desire is for you to reign in life. The more you receive the revelation of the abundance of grace and the gift of righteousness, the more you will experience His abundant provision for every area of your life. Now, we know that faith comes by hearing and hearing the Word of Christ, so keep on hearing the abundance of grace and the gift of righteousness preached. The more you hear, the more you will receive.

*Teach those who are rich in this
world not to be proud and not to trust in their
money, which is so unreliable. Their trust
should be in God, who richly gives us all
we need for our enjoyment.*

—1 TIMOTHY 6:17, NLT

*Blessed is the man who trusts in the Lord,
and whose hope is the Lord. For he shall be like a
tree planted by the waters, which spreads out its
roots by the river, and will not fear when
heat comes; but its leaf will be green, and will
not be anxious in the year of drought, nor
will cease from yielding fruit.*

—JEREMIAH 17:7–8

Trust Completely In Jesus

The Bible tells us clearly not to put our trust in money. Our eyes should never be on money and money should never be our goal. It is unwise to put your trust in uncertain riches.

Rather, turn your eyes upon and put your trust completely in the person of Jesus. Don't make the mistake of pursuing the provision and missing the Provider. The Word declares that it is God who gives and provides us **all that we need for our enjoyment**.

Beloved, when you have Jesus, you have everything. You have peace, righteousness, forgiveness, wisdom, health, power, provision, favor and every blessing. Now, **this** is true prosperity and good success. So anchor yourself on Him and not on material things.

For I determined not to know anything among you except Jesus Christ and Him crucified.

—1 CORINTHIANS 2:2

For I am not ashamed of the gospel of Christ, for it is the power of God to salvation for everyone who believes…

—ROMANS 1:16

Salvation belongs to the Lord. Your blessing is upon Your people.

—PSALM 3:8

It's All About Jesus

Through my television broadcast, a couple in South Dakota received the revelation that the Christian life and walking in God's provision is all about the person of Jesus and His finished work. Wholeheartedly, they began to "focus purely on Jesus alone".

They shared with me that the moment they turned their focus on Jesus, they began to experience breakthrough upon breakthrough. Members of their family were healed from infections, fibromyalgia and pernicious anemia.

Furthermore, their daughter also received a partial scholarship from a Christian university. Two days before she left for school, miraculously, more checks came in that exactly covered the payment for her first year of school. With excitement they shared, "We are amazed at how resting in *Jesus* and what *He* has done has changed our family!"

Beloved, get ready for breakthroughs when you put your trust in Jesus. He loves you!

CHAPTER 2

Come Boldly To
An Abundant God

But Abram said to the king of Sodom, "I have raised my hand to the Lord, God Most High, the Possessor of heaven and earth."

—GENESIS 14:22

For every beast of the forest is Mine, and the cattle on a thousand hills.

—PSALM 50:10

He who did not spare His own Son, but delivered Him up for us all, how shall He not with Him also freely give us all things?

—ROMANS 8:32

Do not be seized with alarm and struck with fear, little flock, for it is your Father's good pleasure to give you the kingdom!

—LUKE 12:32, AMPC

Be Free From Lack

Do you believe that our God is a BIG God of abundance and inexhaustible supply? He is the Possessor of heaven and earth. He is not *El Cheapo*. He is *El Shaddai*—the Almighty, all-sufficient and all-nourishing one! And in Christ, the abundance of God's wisdom, favor, ability, strength and creativity that you need for a successful family, career and ministry, are yours to experience and enjoy.

I want to challenge you to break out of a mentality of lack by choosing to fix your eyes on an abundant God, who has put His unlimited resources at your disposal because you are His beloved child.

What is your lack today? Do you need a job? Do you need more time? Or do you just feel overwhelmed by the demands of family and work? Instead of seeing the lack, start seeing a BIG God providing for you out of His abundance, a job you'll love, wisdom to manage your time and shalom-peace at work and at home.

*The Spirit Himself bears witness with our spirit that
we are children of God, and if children, then heirs—
heirs of God and joint heirs with Christ...*
—**ROMANS 8:16–17**

*Blessed be the God and Father of our Lord Jesus Christ,
who has blessed us with every spiritual blessing in
the heavenly places in Christ.*
—**EPHESIANS 1:3**

*His divine power has given us everything we need for life
and godliness through our knowledge of Him who
called us by His own glory and goodness.*
—**2 PETER 1:3, NIV**

*If you then, being evil, know how to give good gifts to
your children, how much more will your Father
who is in heaven give good things
to those who ask Him!*
—**MATTHEW 7:11**

It's Time To Change Your Mind

I'm too young. I'm too old. I don't have the relevant experience. They're hiring only college graduates. If you're looking for a job and your mind is gripped by such thoughts, then you're already defeated by your thoughts before you even step out for an interview.

It's time to change your mind. As God's child, you are His heir and a joint heir with Christ. This means that you have the same unclouded favor that Jesus has. So step out in faith and expect His favor to open doors for you and give you the job you desire, regardless of your natural limitations.

A lady in her mid-fifties in my congregation, after hearing me share on this, changed her mind. She decided to put her trust in the Lord's unmerited favor, got her résumé ready and sent it out by faith. That very week, she was called for interviews by two different companies, which led to two job offers! She picked one and has been gainfully employed for the last five years!

GOD *who owns the universe* is your **HEAVENLY FATHER.**

You are
God's CHILD,
His **HEIR** *and a*
JOINT HEIR
with Jesus.

For you know the grace of our Lord Jesus Christ,
that though He was rich, yet for your sakes He
became poor, that you through His
poverty might become rich.
—2 CORINTHIANS 8:9

After they had nailed Him to the cross, the
soldiers gambled for His clothes by throwing dice.
—MATTHEW 27:35, NLT

…You shall lend to many nations, but you shall
not borrow. And the Lord will make you
the head and not the tail…
—DEUTERONOMY 28:12–13

The Divine Exchange

The apostle Paul tells us in 2 Corinthians 8:9 that, for our sakes, Jesus became poor, so that we through His poverty might be made rich. At the cross, Jesus took on all our sin and poverty. He was humiliated, spat upon and stripped naked. The Roman soldiers even gambled for His clothes.

The One who fed more than 5,000 people, gave fishermen a net-breaking, boat-sinking load of fish, and who placed the gold, diamonds and rubies in the earth, took your place of poverty at the cross, just so that *you* can take His place of abundance. A divine exchange occurred at Calvary—your sin for His righteousness and your poverty for His provision.

My friend, Jesus is the reason you can be the head and not the tail, above only and not beneath, the lender and not the borrower. HE is the reason you can be blessed to be a blessing!

*Therefore do not worry, saying, "What shall we eat?"
or "What shall we drink?" or "What shall we wear?"
For after all these things the Gentiles seek. For
your heavenly Father knows that you
need all these things.*

—**Matthew 6:31–32**

*Blessed shall be the fruit of your body, the produce
of your ground and the increase of your herds, the
increase of your cattle and the offspring of your flocks.
Blessed shall be your basket and your kneading bowl.
Blessed shall you be when you come in, and blessed
shall you be when you go out. The Lord will cause
your enemies who rise against you to be defeated
before your face; they shall come out against you one
way and flee before you seven ways. The Lord will
command the blessing on you in your storehouses
and in all to which you set your hand...*

—**Deuteronomy 28:4–8**

God Is A Practical God

Our God is a **practical** God, who is interested in providing for your practical daily needs. Take a look at Jesus throughout the four Gospel accounts.

To those who were hungry, He provided food by multiplying the loaves and fish. To the fishermen who toiled all night and caught nothing, He gave them more than a boatload of fish. Jesus didn't stop there—whoever encountered Him received from Him what they lacked. He healed the broken hearted and gave sight to the blind. The sick who came to Him were all healed. Even the dead received His resurrection life!

My friend, Jesus is the same, yesterday, today and forever! He is still providing. So whatever you need today, whether it is wisdom, favor, healing or divine strength, go to Him. He is a practical God.

*And this same God who takes care of me will
supply all your needs from His glorious riches,
which have been given to us in Christ Jesus.*
—**PHILIPPIANS 4:19, NLT**

*Blessed be the Lord, who daily loads us with
benefits, the God of our salvation!*
—**PSALM 68:19**

*A man's gift makes room for him, and
brings him before great men.*
—**PROVERBS 18:16**

*The soul of a lazy man desires, and has
nothing; but the soul of the diligent
shall be made rich.*
—**PROVERBS 13:4**

God's Grace Is Always Supplying

When Jesus cried out, "It is finished!" the wall of sin that separated us from God crumbled, and God unleashed a flood tide of His grace upon us. That grace is still flowing toward us today, supplying whatever we need in this life, daily loading us with benefits!

My friend, the essence of God's grace is SUPPLY. When you are conscious of His supply, instead of the demands of the world, you are under His grace. That's when you will see His abundant provision for every need and situation.

So if you're having trouble finding a job, beyond trusting God for employment, see the Lord stirring up the dormant giftings and abilities that He has already placed in you. As you hone these gifts, the Word of God declares that your gifts will unlock doors of opportunities in due season and cause you to stand before great men. Don't just believe you'll be employed, believe God to also prepare, grow and develop you for a position of influence in your industry!

One of His disciples, Andrew, Simon Peter's brother, said to Him, "There is a lad here who has five barley loaves and two small fish, but what are they among so many?" Then Jesus said, "Make the people sit down." Now there was much grass in the place. So the men sat down, in number about five thousand. And Jesus took the loaves, and when He had given thanks He distributed them to the disciples, and the disciples to those sitting down; and likewise of the fish, as much as they wanted. So when they were filled, He said to His disciples, "Gather up the fragments that remain, so that nothing is lost." Therefore they gathered them up, and filled twelve baskets with the fragments of the five barley loaves which were left over by those who had eaten.

—JOHN 6:8–13

Place It In His Hands

When Jesus saw the five loaves and two little fish, unlike His disciples, He didn't see the naturally impossible **demand** placed on Him—to feed 5,000 men (not including the women and children) with a boy's small lunch. He saw the supernatural **supply** in His Father's kingdom.

The result? Not only were the people fed till they were stuffed, there were also 12 baskets full of leftovers!

My friend, are you facing a situation of insufficiency today? Perhaps you can't find enough time to get your work done, as well as spend quality time with your family. Why not put your time in Jesus' hands and, as with the five loaves and two little fish, allow Him to multiply it? Jesus will give you the wisdom on how best to use your time.

Try it for yourself. Bring your little to Jesus! He will multiply whatever little you place in His hands with plenty left over!

*When He had come down from the mountain,
great multitudes followed Him. And behold, a
leper came and worshiped Him, saying, "Lord, if
You are willing, You can make me clean." Then
Jesus put out His hand and touched him, saying,
"I am willing; be cleansed." Immediately his
leprosy was cleansed.*

—MATTHEW 8:1–3

*Now to Him who is able to do exceedingly
abundantly above all that we ask or think,
according to the power that works in us.*

—EPHESIANS 3:20

Beyond All Expectations

When the Lord blesses you, He blesses you beyond what you expect. In the healing of the leper, Jesus reached out and touched the leper, saying, "I am willing; be cleansed." And immediately, the man was healed.

My friend, did you notice that Jesus *touched* the leper first before He healed him? I love these little gestures of Jesus! That simple touch restored a sense of humanity and dignity to the man who had not been touched for a long time. Because of his unclean and physically repulsive condition, no one wanted to be close to him, much less touch him.

Jesus knew that the leper needed more than just physical healing, so He gave above and beyond what the leper had hoped for. Beloved, that's the love and over-supplying grace of your Savior! What is your lack today? Know beyond any doubt that Jesus' provision will exceed all your expectations!

Ask BIG.
Dream BIG.

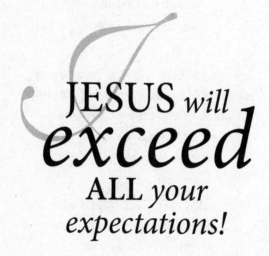

JESUS *will* *exceed* ALL *your* *expectations!*

*...I came that they may have and enjoy life,
and have it in abundance (to the
full, till it overflows).*

—JOHN 10:10, AMPC

*Jesus said to him, "Thomas, because you
have seen Me, you have believed. Blessed
are those who have not seen and
yet have believed."*

—JOHN 20:29

*...let them say continually, "Let the Lord be
magnified, who has pleasure in the
prosperity of His servant."*

—PSALM 35:27

*He who has a slack hand becomes poor, but
the hand of the diligent makes rich.*

—PROVERBS 10:4

The Abundant God

A lady in my congregation heard me preach on John 10:10—how Jesus came that we may have life and have it more abundantly. From that moment, the revelation of an abundant God began to resonate within her.

You see, as an orphan, this lady had grown up in extreme poverty. However, when she began meditating on her abundant God, things began to change. She began to have big dreams and started a company to pursue those dreams. Today, her little company is a behemoth public-listed company and a world leader in her industry. Her personal net worth is in the hundreds of millions.

One of the most humble people you will ever meet, she always has the phrase, "the abundant God", on her lips. When people ask her for the secret to her success, she would simply share with a gentle smile, "My abundant God has blessed me." My friend, be encouraged, and begin to see God as your ABUNDANT God today!

*Now it happened on another Sabbath, also,
that He entered the synagogue and taught.
And a man was there whose right hand was
withered…And when He had looked around
at them all, He said to the man, "Stretch out
your hand." And he did so, and his hand
was restored as whole as the other.*

—LUKE 6:6, 10

*Remember the Lord your God. He is the one
who gives you power to be successful…*

—DEUTERONOMY 8:18, NLT

Restoring The Power To Provide

With each of the Lord's blessings you experience, be encouraged to know that many more blessings are coming your way. Just as there are many seeds in one fruit, so each of Jesus' blessings contains many seeds that will go on to provide many more blessings for you and your family.

Consider Jesus' healing of the man with the withered arm. The Gospel of Luke tells us that it was the man's *right hand* that was withered. Now, the right hand is a picture of strength and provision. This man had lost not only his strength, but also his ability to provide! So when Jesus healed this man's right hand, He not only performed a healing miracle, but He also restored to this man the power and the ability to provide for himself and his family! Hallelujah!

Is your strength and ability to provide "withered" today? Jesus says to you, "Stretch out your hand, be healed and completely restored with the power to provide for yourself and your family!"

*And Jesus took the loaves, and when He
had given thanks He distributed them to the
disciples, and the disciples to those sitting down;
and likewise of the fish, as much as they wanted.
So when they were filled, He said to His disciples,
"Gather up the fragments that remain, so that
nothing is lost." Therefore they gathered them
up, and filled twelve baskets with the fragments
of the five barley loaves which were left over
by those who had eaten.*

—JOHN 6:11–13

*God can do anything, you know—far more
than you could ever imagine or guess or request
in your wildest dreams! He does it...by
working within us, His Spirit deeply
and gently within us.*

—EPHESIANS 3:20, THE MESSAGE

You Cannot Exhaust His Supply

Let's look again at the miracle that Jesus performed in the feeding of the 5,000. This miracle is the only miracle Jesus performed that is recorded in all of the four Gospel accounts! This tells us that Jesus wants us to draw out all the hidden revelations in this miracle. Are you ready?

Now, did you notice how John records that the people ate "as much as they wanted" until "they were FILLED"? In other words, they ate and ate until they could eat no more! **Everyone ate to his heart's content** and still there was plenty left over—12 baskets full, to be precise!

God's supply of provision will always exceed your demand! He is such a BIG God, there is nothing He cannot do. My friend, don't look to the world to supply your lack. Be wise—don't touch easy loans with exorbitant interest rates hidden in the fine print, and become trapped in a financially sapping cycle of debt. Look to Jesus, His ways and His supply that never fails!

...Elisha said to her, "What shall I do for you? Tell me, what do you have in the house?" And she said, "Your maidservant has nothing in the house but a jar of oil." Then he said, "Go, borrow vessels from everywhere, from all your neighbors—empty vessels; do not gather just a few. And when you have come in, you shall shut the door behind you and your sons; then pour it into all those vessels, and set aside the full ones." So she went from him and shut the door behind her and her sons, who brought the vessels to her; and she poured it out. Now it came to pass, when the vessels were full, that she said to her son, "Bring me another vessel." And he said to her, "There is not another vessel." So the oil ceased. Then she came and told the man of God. And he said, "Go, sell the oil and pay your debt; and you and your sons live on the rest."

—2 KINGS 4:2–7

Clear Your Debts First

Elisha told a poor widow to get as many empty vessels as she could, and pour her last jar of oil into the vessels. She did as told and miraculously, the oil kept flowing. It stopped only when she ran out of vessels. Elisha then told her to sell the oil, pay her debt and live prudently on the surplus.

My friend, I want you to see two important things here. Firstly, the supply stopped **only when the demand on God's supply stopped**. I want to encourage you to never stop looking to Jesus for your supply.

Secondly, if you are in debt, your first priority is to settle your debt—Elisha told the widow, "Sell the oil and **pay your debt**." And when you have cleared your debt, learn to live within your current means. Heed the practical wisdom in God's Word without which you will not be able to *contain* His provision.

Jesus' supply is
INEXHAUSTIBLE.

Look to Him
for your *supply.*

One of His disciples, Andrew, Simon Peter's brother, said to Him, "There is a lad here who has five barley loaves and two small fish, but what are they among so many?"

—**JOHN 6:8**

Do not despise these small beginnings, for the Lord rejoices to see the work begin, to see the plumb line in Zerubbabel's hand.

—**ZECHARIAH 4:10, NLT**

…God chose the weak things of the world to shame the strong. He chose the lowly things of this world and the despised things…to nullify the things that are, so that no one may boast before Him.

—**1 CORINTHIANS 1:27–29, NIV**

The hand of the diligent will rule, but the lazy man will be put to forced labor.

—**PROVERBS 12:24**

Do Not Despise Humble Beginnings

It's interesting to see how God never despises the little things.

When the boy brought his five loaves and two fish, the disciple Andrew scoffed, condescendingly patted the boy on his head and said to Jesus, "What are they among so many?" In direct contrast, God did not despise the boy's small lunch.

My friend, don't despise the little things that you have right now. See them as your very own "five loaves and two fish" even when people around you mock and belittle you. Learn to disregard such people and lay your little before Jesus. While you and I have no power to multiply, Jesus certainly does!

So whatever you are building right now in your career, your ministry, or your business, don't despise the day of small, humble and seemingly insignificant beginnings. Involve Jesus and allow His provision of favor, wisdom and power to multiply and grow the little things in your hands.

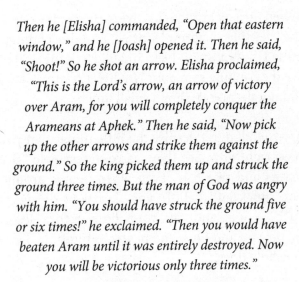

Then he [Elisha] commanded, "Open that eastern window," and he [Joash] opened it. Then he said, "Shoot!" So he shot an arrow. Elisha proclaimed, "This is the Lord's arrow, an arrow of victory over Aram, for you will completely conquer the Arameans at Aphek." Then he said, "Now pick up the other arrows and strike them against the ground." So the king picked them up and struck the ground three times. But the man of God was angry with him. "You should have struck the ground five or six times!" he exclaimed. "Then you would have beaten Aram until it was entirely destroyed. Now you will be victorious only three times."

—2 KINGS 13:17–19, NLT

Complete Victory Is Yours

God was willing to give him complete victory. All he had to do was be bold in claiming and taking it. You would think that that was an easy thing to do, wouldn't you?

But King Joash didn't go for broke. When the prophet Elisha told him that God would give him victory over the Arameans, and told him to strike some arrows on the ground to represent the extent of his victory, King Joash struck the arrows on the ground only three times, when he could have done it twice as many times. Unfortunately, that meant that instead of destroying Aram completely, King Joash would enjoy only three victories over the Arameans.

Beloved, God is more than willing to give you complete victory in every area of challenge today. Because Christ has secured for you every provision you need in life, you don't have to settle for partial healing, or for His help and wisdom only for "big" problems. Boldly press on in faith until you see *complete victory* over *all* your challenges!

*Now it happened as they went that He entered
a certain village; and a certain woman named
Martha welcomed Him into her house. And she
had a sister called Mary, who also sat at Jesus' feet
and heard His word. But Martha was distracted
with much serving, and she approached Him and
said, "Lord, do You not care that my sister has left
me to serve alone? Therefore tell her to help me."
And Jesus answered and said to her, "Martha,
Martha, you are worried and troubled about
many things. But one thing is needed, and Mary
has chosen that good part, which will not
be taken away from her."*

—LUKE 10:38–42

*Jesus replied, "I am the bread of life. Whoever
comes to Me will never be hungry again. Whoever
believes in Me will never be thirsty."*

—JOHN 6:35, NLT

Take From Him

Martha was busy **serving** Jesus while her sister, Mary, sat at His feet and **drew** from Him words of life. Martha didn't like it that Mary wasn't helping her, so she complained about it to Jesus. Who do you think Jesus defended? Mary!

My friend, many believers think that it's better to give than to receive. Now, that's true in our relationships with *people*. But when it comes to our relationship with the *Lord*, it's better to RECEIVE from Him than to try to give to Him! Jesus describes Himself as the "bread of life", in essence telling us that He wants us to partake of Him and receive from Him all the nourishment, strength, healing, provision and abundant life we can take!

Our Lord loves it when we take from Him. That's why Mary pleased Jesus. Beloved, I encourage you to be a Mary today. Our loving heavenly Father loves it when we draw from His unending reservoir of strength, wisdom, favor, peace and life!

*...you are complete in Him, who is the
head of all principality and power.*

—**Colossians 2:10**

*To them God willed to make known what
are the riches of the glory of this mystery
among the Gentiles: which is Christ in
you, the hope of glory.*

—**Colossians 1:27**

*Delight yourself also in the Lord, and He
shall give you the desires of your heart.*

—**Psalm 37:4**

Find Your Completion In Christ

Many people are in financial debt today because, instead of finding their security, identity and esteem in Christ and Christ alone, they are trying to find it in material things. So they end up buying things that they don't need to impress people who really don't care!

This erroneous mindset leads to the destructive habit of folks spending beyond their means, making only partial payments on their monthly credit card bills, and overextending themselves with mortgages they cannot afford and car loans they cannot service. Then, they end up asking God why there is no provision for their debts.

Beloved, being caught in this destructive habit and debt cycle is not God's heart for His precious children. Let's understand that having *more things* doesn't complete us. Only Jesus can fill that vacuum. Find your security and completion in Christ. You have a treasure in you, One far more precious than anything money can buy. Anchor your security and identity in Jesus!

…and the borrower is servant to the lender.
—PROVERBS 22:7

*Owe no one anything except to love
one another…*
—ROMANS 13:8

*The Lord will open to you His good treasure,
the heavens, to give the rain to your land in its
season, and to bless all the work of your hand.
You shall lend to many nations, but you
shall not borrow.*
—DEUTERONOMY 28:12

*The plans of the diligent lead surely to plenty, but
those of everyone who is hasty, surely to poverty.*
—PROVERBS 21:5

*And my God shall supply all your need according
to His riches in glory by Christ Jesus.*
—PHILIPPIANS 4:19

Blessed To Be Givers

God blesses you and provides abundantly for you and your family so that you can always find yourself in a place to give and be a blessing.

He wants you to be a lender, rather than a borrower who is constantly struggling to pay off his debts, so that you can be a blessing to many.

My friend, keep looking to His finished work to provide for all your needs. Don't succumb to the lure to borrow unwisely. Don't take up easy credit loans which make available to you thousands of dollars (that are not yours) to spend, and then struggle just to pay off the high interest later. This will only take a toll on your peace of mind, health and family relationships.

Beloved, be wise. Look to Christ for your provision and by His grace be diligent in all that you do. You'll be so blessed you can't help but be a blessing!

*Jabez was more honorable than his brothers.
His mother had named him Jabez, saying, "I
gave birth to him in pain." Jabez cried out to
the God of Israel, "Oh, that You would bless me
and enlarge my territory! Let Your hand be with
me, and keep me from harm so that I will be free
from pain." And God granted his request.*

—1 CHRONICLES 4:9–10, NIV

*Let us therefore come boldly to the throne of
grace, that we may obtain mercy and find grace
to help in time of need.*

—HEBREWS 4:16

*If any of you lacks wisdom, let him ask of God,
who gives to all liberally and without reproach,
and it will be given to him.*

—JAMES 1:5

Pray The Prayer Of Jabez!

There was once a boy named Sorrow. His mother gave him that name because she bore him in pain. You can imagine that with a name like that, it's quite likely no one liked him.

So do you know what Sorrow, otherwise known as Jabez in the Old Testament, did? He called on the God of Israel to BLESS him! "Oh, that You would **bless** me and **enlarge** my territory…" That's asking God for provision and increase. He also asked for God's hand to be with him so that he would be blessed in all that he did and be protected from harm. God not only granted Jabez his request, but He also considered Jabez more **honorable** than his brothers!

Today, do the honorable thing—ask the Lord to increase and enlarge the favor, wisdom, abilities and opportunities for growth you currently have *to a whole new level*. Ask Him for divine wisdom to protect you from making unwise decisions that lead to painful consequences.

...Jesus said to him [Peter], "...lest we offend them, go to the sea, cast in a hook, and take the fish that comes up first. And when you have opened its mouth, you will find a piece of money; take that and give it to them for Me and you."

—**MATTHEW 17:26–27**

...Jesus sent two disciples, saying to them, "Go into the village opposite you, and immediately you will find a donkey tied, and a colt with her. Loose them and bring them to Me. And if anyone says anything to you, you shall say, 'The Lord has need of them,' and immediately he will send them."

—**MATTHEW 21:1–3**

And He sent out two of His disciples and said to them, "Go into the city, and a man will meet you carrying a pitcher of water; follow him. Wherever he goes in, say to the master of the house, 'The Teacher says, "Where is the guest room in which I may eat the Passover with My disciples?"' Then he will show you a large upper room, furnished and prepared; there make ready for us."

—**MARK 14:13–15**

Right Place, Right Time

Whatever you need, Jesus knows *where* you can get it, and *whom* you can get it from. Jesus can position you at the right place at the right time!

When Peter wanted to pay the temple tax, Jesus told him to get it from the first fish that he would catch in the sea. Then, when Jesus needed a donkey to ride into Jerusalem, He told two of His disciples which village to get it from. When Jesus needed a place to eat the Passover with His disciples, He gave two of His disciples specific instructions on who to meet and follow, and what to say to the master of the house, who had already furnished and prepared a large upper room!

My friend, isn't it wonderful to know that Jesus knows what you need and has already gone ahead into your future and made provision for your good success? As you put your trust and rest in His heart of love, His peace will lead you to do the right thing at the right time, at the right place!

Jesus is *pleased*
when you
DEPEND
on **HIM** and
TAKE from **HIM**
all that you need.

With man, it is more blessed to ***give.***

With GOD, it is more blessed to ***receive.***

*I will make you a great nation; I will bless
you and make your name great; and
you shall be a blessing.*

—**GENESIS 12:2**

*So let each one give as he purposes in his
heart, not grudgingly or of necessity; for God
loves a cheerful giver. And God is able to
make all grace abound toward you, that you,
always having all sufficiency in all things,
may have an abundance for
every good work.*

—**2 CORINTHIANS 9:7–8**

*…"Surely blessing I will bless you, and
multiplying I will multiply you."*

—**HEBREWS 6:14**

Blessed To Be A Blessing

Listen to the words that God pronounced over Abraham: "I will bless you and make your name great; and you shall be a blessing".

My friend, as you trust God to walk more and more in the fullness of Abraham's blessing, have a revelation that He blesses you because He loves you, and gives to you the privilege of being a practical extension of His love to your community, your country and beyond.

God's financial provision is for a divine purpose. Don't use people and love money. Instead, use money to love people! When it comes to our relationship with people, it is always more blessed to give than to receive. Have an abundant eye and heart, look around for people in need and bless them. Let your light so shine before all men for the glory of the name of Jesus Christ!

Today, see His abundant grace abounding toward you and your family so that you will have an abundance for every good work!

CHAPTER 3

*Boldly Receive
And Reign*

*In Him we have redemption through His blood,
the forgiveness of sins, according to the
riches of His grace.*

—EPHESIANS 1:7

*He has delivered us from the power of darkness
and conveyed us into the kingdom of the Son of
His love, in whom we have redemption through
His blood, the forgiveness of sins.*

—COLOSSIANS 1:13–14

*And you, being dead in your trespasses and the
uncircumcision of your flesh, He has made alive
together with Him, having forgiven
you all trespasses.*

—COLOSSIANS 2:13

Jesus—Our Greatest Provision

As we meditate on the provision promises that our heavenly Father has laid out for us in His Word, let's take a moment to reflect on the finished work of Jesus.

At the cross, Jesus gave of Himself completely and made a provision for the forgiveness of our sins that no one else could. He chose to lay down His life in exchange for ours. All our sins, failures and mistakes are forever washed away by the precious blood shed at Calvary! Truly, in Christ we have redemption through His blood, the forgiveness of sins, "**according to the riches of His grace**".

My friend, God's grace toward you is bountiful and rich. Today, receive His grace, His forgiveness, His love and His mercy in a fresh and powerful way. It is not material wealth that makes one rich. Having Jesus is your greatest wealth!

The next day John saw Jesus coming toward him, and said, "Behold! The Lamb of God who takes away the sin of the world!"

—JOHN 1:29

With His own blood—not the blood of goats and calves—He entered the Most Holy Place once for all time and secured our redemption forever.

—HEBREWS 9:12, NLT

And my God shall supply all your need according to His riches in glory by Christ Jesus.

—PHILIPPIANS 4:19

Receive The Provision Of Forgiveness Daily

Many people think that forgiveness is a basic teaching, that it is something you learn when you are a new believer and then you move on to more "complex" truths in God's Word.

My friend, I submit to you that there is nothing basic about having a deep and abiding revelation of forgiveness. In fact, I believe that if you want to live the Christ-life and walk in the fullness of His divine provision, you need to meditate on His forgiveness daily. Personally, that is what I endeavor to do every single day when I partake of the Holy Communion in the privacy of my study.

I take the bread in my hand and thank Jesus for His provision of health, healing and wholeness for me. Then, I hold up the cup and thank my Savior for the provision of His blood that washes me whiter than snow and makes me righteous! Beloved, look to the cross and see how He has made possible every provision you need!

I write to you, little children, because your sins are forgiven you for His name's sake.

—1 JOHN 2:12

For I will be merciful to their unrighteousness, and their sins and their lawless deeds I will remember no more.

—HEBREWS 8:12

…He adds, "Their sins and their lawless deeds I will remember no more."

—HEBREWS 10:17

God Does Not Remember Your Sins

My friend, do you believe today that God does not remember your sins? This is a truth that our finite human minds struggle to comprehend.

How can an omnipotent, omniscient and omnipresent God not remember our sins? An allpowerful, all-knowing, all-present God should rightly be able to remember every single detail of every sin that we have committed. But that's not what the Word of God says. God declares, "For I will be merciful to their unrighteousness, and their sins and their lawless deeds **I will remember no more.**" I believe many believers are fearful to come close to God today and receive what they need from Him because they don't believe that God truly remembers their sins no more.

My friend, simply believe God's Word, that through the provision of Jesus' sacrifice, God indeed remembers your sins no more! Start living without the cloud of guilt, shame, condemnation and judgment over your head. Stand bold and righteous in Christ and expect to receive His best!

There is NO sin
standing in the way of
your blessing
that JESUS
didn't take care of.

'Your sins I will
NEVER,
BY NO MEANS,
remember.'

—God

For He made Him who knew no sin to be sin for us, that we might become the righteousness of God in Him.

—2 CORINTHIANS 5:21

For the eyes of the Lord are on the righteous, and His ears are open to their prayers…

—1 PETER 3:12

…He hears the prayer of the righteous.

—PROVERBS 15:29

The righteous cry out, and the Lord hears, and delivers them out of all their troubles.

—PSALM 34:17

…The earnest prayer of a righteous person has great power and produces wonderful results.

—JAMES 5:16, NLT

Your Prayers Produce Wonderful Results

When Jesus was crucified on the cross, not only did He wash away all your sins with His precious blood, but He also gave you His very own RIGHTEOUSNESS as a gift. Do you know that you can never lose this righteousness? Your righteousness is a gift from Jesus because it is entirely dependent on *His* perfect performance and *His* perfect obedience, not yours.

So my friend, because you are forever righteous in Christ, God *hears* your prayers every time you pray. Apostle James tells us that the earnest prayer of a righteous man—that's YOU—"produces wonderful results". Not just plain results, but *wonderful* results!

What provision do you need today, righteous one? Favor for an interview, wisdom to clear your debts, healing for your children? As a righteous man or woman of God, boldly ask Jesus for what you need in prayer!

❀

Blessings are on the head of the righteous...
—PROVERBS 10:6

...the desire of the righteous will be granted.
—PROVERBS 10:24

The hope of the righteous will be gladness...
—PROVERBS 10:28

*In the house of the righteous there is
much treasure...*
—PROVERBS 15:6

*For You, O Lord, will bless the righteous;
with favor You will surround him
as with a shield.*
—PSALM 5:12

❀

God Blesses You, The Righteous

Whenever you find a promise or blessing for the righteous in the Bible, grab hold of it by saying, "Father, I receive this blessing in Jesus' name!"

Let me show you how to practice this. When you read in Proverbs 10:6 that blessings are on the head of the righteous, say, "Thank You, Father, this promise is for ME because I have been made **righteous** through faith in Jesus and His finished work!"

So every day, instead of fearing that lack will devour you, expect God's provision and blessings to hunt you down and surround you! Expect good things to happen to you. Say, "Father, I thank You that Your blessings crown my head. Your bountiful provisions are upon me and my household!"

Beloved, the more you begin to believe and speak words of abundance, provision and increase, the more you will experience the full blessings of the righteous!

For if by the one man's offense death reigned through the one, much more those who receive abundance of grace and of the gift of righteousness will reign in life through the One, Jesus Christ.

—**Romans 5:17**

The thief does not come except to steal, and to kill, and to destroy. I have come that they may have life, and that they may have it more abundantly.

—**John 10:10**

Beloved, I wish above all things that thou mayest prosper and be in health, even as thy soul prospereth.

—**3 John 1:2, kjv**

The Righteous Reign!

God's Word declares that those who receive abundance of grace and the gift of righteousness will reign in life. Beloved, it is clear that your heavenly Father's heart is to see you reign in life!

You are not reigning when you are riddled with credit card debt, suffering lack or struggling to provide for your family. If that is where you are today, don't give up! Look to Jesus and begin to actively receive the abundance of grace and the gift of righteousness daily!

His grace will give you the wisdom and strength to change your spending habits and make good decisions to get out of debt. His grace will open doors of favor for new employment opportunities and provide avenues for you to improve and develop the gifts that He has placed in you so that you can secure a better job in the future. Beloved, believe that you are destined to reign over all your debts and financial lack!

You are
destined to reign
over **all** *debt and*
financial lack.

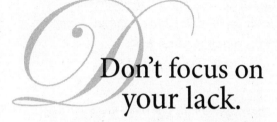

Don't focus on your lack.

Focus on *God's* **ABUNDANT** *supply* and *expect to experience it.*

But now the righteousness of God apart from the law is revealed…even the righteousness of God, through faith in Jesus Christ, to all and on all who believe…being justified freely by His grace through the redemption that is in Christ Jesus.

—**ROMANS 3:21–24**

For if, by the trespass of the one man, death reigned through that one man, how much more will those who receive God's abundant provision of grace and of the gift of righteousness reign in life through the one Man, Jesus Christ.

—**ROMANS 5:17, NIV**

…Freely you have received…

—**MATTHEW 10:8**

And if by grace, then it is no longer of works; otherwise grace is no longer grace. But if it is of works, it is no longer grace; otherwise work is no longer work.

—**ROMANS 11:6**

The Vast Ocean Of His Abundant Supply

In Romans 5:17, Paul gives us the key to reigning in life. It is found in RECEIVING the abundance of God's grace and His gift of righteousness.

Something happens when you receive the abundance of God's grace, stop depending on your own efforts and lean wholly upon **His grace**. The moment you surrender and say, "Lord, I cannot, but You can. Today, I rest in Your unmerited favor," whatever demand that is upon you disappears into the vast ocean of His abundant supply.

Many times, as I'm driving to church on Sunday morning, I feel the demand to preach a good message. The demand is real—more than 20,000 people in my congregation show up expecting to be well fed! That's when I turn to Jesus and receive His abundance of grace. I say to Him, "Lord, today, You are my guest speaker! I rest in You. You speak. You feed them. You provide! You take over and I will watch You in action!" The moment I let go, His grace and His supply rush in! Hallelujah!

...Those who are righteous...do not fear bad news; they confidently trust the Lord to care for them. They are confident and fearless and can face their foes triumphantly.

—PSALM 112:6–8, NLT

He who did not spare His own Son, but delivered Him up for us all, how shall He not with Him also freely give us all things?

—ROMANS 8:32

Now faith is the substance of things hoped for, the evidence of things not seen.

—HEBREWS 11:1

...as you have believed, so let it be done for you...

—MATTHEW 8:13

Start The Day Expecting Good

Wake up every day expecting good. Keep your thoughts and mind positive, full of joy, full of hope and full of anticipation of all the good things God has in store for you, His beloved!

Spring up from your bed, stand in front of your mirror and boldly declare, "I am the disciple whom Jesus loves. I am the apple of His eye. Everything I do and touch shall be blessed! The Lord's wisdom, favor and provision flow mightily in and through me. Amen!"

When you do this, you are accessing the Lord's abundant provision for you, and all the stress, worries, negative emotions and anxieties will fade away.

Perhaps today, you have to make an important presentation to your biggest client, or go for the final interview for a job you really want. Perhaps you are way behind the curve in completing an important project at work. Whatever the demands on you, start the day expecting good and to see His provision flow!

Reigning in life
is *not achieved*
through self-effort,
but **RECEIVED**
by grace through faith.

Grace Transforms

I received a letter from a young lady in Virginia, and want to share her powerful testimony with you in her own words:

In college, I began to have a losing battle with depression...Things were so bad that I couldn't even get up in the mornings because I was so tormented in my mind. Therapy and medication didn't help as I battled with this painful nightmare for seven long years. Then, my mom gave me your book, Destined To Reign. When I began to accept God's love for me and trust Jesus and His finished work, I was totally and miraculously healed! After reading the book, every day, I would just say, "Lord, I am not even going to try today. You live the victorious life for me. I cannot overcome these thoughts on my own, but I can rest in You." I now live a life of joy and peace that I never imagined was possible!

Beloved, what are you struggling with today? Give it up to the Lord, and let His provision of grace flood your area of need. Only His grace can transform you from the inside out and lead you to live a life of victory!

*This left Jacob all alone in the camp, and a Man
came and wrestled with him until the dawn began
to break…He touched Jacob's hip and wrenched
it out of its socket…"Your name will no longer be
Jacob," the Man told him. "From now on you will
be called Israel…Then He blessed Jacob there.*

—**GENESIS 32:24–29, NLT**

*"My brother, I have plenty," Esau answered. "Keep
what you have for yourself." But Jacob insisted,
"No, if I have found favor with you, please accept
this gift from me…for God has been very gracious
to me. I have more than enough."…*

—**GENESIS 33:9–11, NLT**

Grace Flows When You Stop Struggling

Most people would have given up on Jacob, the scheming deceiver and manipulator. But not God.

One night, while attempting to appease the brother he had stolen from, Jacob met the Lord. He grabbed hold of the Lord and for hours, tried to wrestle a blessing from Him. What did the Lord do? He touched Jacob's hip socket and put it out of joint, so that Jacob wound up helpless before the Lord.

The Lord changed Jacob that night. He showed Jacob how it was only when Jacob's grabbing and wrestling finally stopped that His grace was able to flow. That night, God changed Jacob's name from "deceiver" to "prince" (Israel), and added to him blessings that were beyond his own efforts.

You see, we cannot try to wrestle blessings from God. It is when we give up on our scheming, deceiving and manipulating to get ahead in life, and completely trust His grace alone that His provision flows unabated.

There is therefore now no condemnation for those who are in Christ Jesus.

—**ROMANS 8:1, NASB**

Don't you see how wonderfully kind, tolerant, and patient God is with you? Does this mean nothing to you? Can't you see that His kindness is intended to turn you from your sin?

—**ROMANS 2:4, NLT**

Awake to righteousness, and sin not…

—**1 CORINTHIANS 15:34, KJV**

For sin shall not have dominion over you, for you are not under law but under grace.

—**ROMANS 6:14**

Delivered Through A Revelation Of Righteousness

I give thanks to the Lord for all the testimonies I've received from precious lives touched by Jesus. Here's one from a brother in Australia, who wrote to me to share how he had been delivered from multiple addictions as he started to hear and receive the revelation of his righteousness in Christ.

I have just given up smoking by doing what you've taught in your books and DVDs—becoming conscious of and confessing my righteousness in Christ—whenever I was tempted to smoke. I have also been set free from 20 years of drug and alcohol abuse, and am free of paranoid thoughts. I couldn't give them up through my own efforts, but through Christ I have. Praise Jesus for His overcoming grace!

My friend, God's provision covers all aspects of life, including deliverance from long-term addictions. When you continually receive God's gifts of abundant grace, righteousness and no condemnation in Christ, you *will* walk in His power to reign over every addiction or condition holding you captive today!

Blessings crown the head of the righteous…
—PROVERBS 10:6, NIV

I will greatly rejoice in the Lord, my soul shall be joyful in my God; for He has clothed me with the garments of salvation, He has covered me with the robe of righteousness…
—ISAIAH 61:10

"In righteousness you shall be established; you shall be far from oppression, for you shall not fear; and from terror, for it shall not come near you…No weapon formed against you shall prosper, and every tongue which rises against you in judgment you shall condemn. This is the heritage of the servants of the Lord, and their righteousness is from Me," says the Lord.
—ISAIAH 54:14, 17

A Robust Revelation Of Your Righteousness

I really want you to reign in all areas of life by receiving a robust revelation of your righteousness in Christ. You grow in this revelation the more you hear about what Jesus has accomplished for you at the cross.

The Bible tells us that blessings crown the head of the righteous. So the larger the revelation of your righteousness in Christ and the more you are established in it, the more you will see God's blessings manifest in your life.

Let me put it another way: See the robe of righteousness that God has already clothed you with having pockets labeled "favor", "healing", "deliverance", "provision", "wisdom", "family blessings" and so on. The more conscious you are of this robe on you, the more you will experience the good gifts that come with it and live a purposeful and fulfilling life—a life where you have more than enough to bless others as well!

The more you
believe
that you are
righteous
in Christ...

T...the more you will experience *the* blessings *of the righteous.*

Therefore do not worry, saying, "What shall we eat?" or "What shall we drink?" or "What shall we wear?" For after all these things the Gentiles seek. For your heavenly Father knows that you need all these things. But seek first the kingdom of God and His righteousness, and all these things shall be added to you.

—MATTHEW 6:31–33

The way of the wicked is an abomination to the Lord, but He loves him who follows righteousness.

—PROVERBS 15:9

…If God is for us, who can be against us?

—ROMANS 8:31

Seek First Jesus' Righteousness

I encourage you to take some time each day to get the revelation of your righteousness in Christ deep into your spirit. Meditate on it and declare it every day. It will put courage in your heart and bring an unshakable peace to your soul. It will energize your faith when you pray and give you a confident expectation to receive good things from your heavenly Father.

I believe that's why our heavenly Father, in knowing the things that we need daily, tells us not to worry about them. What are we supposed to do then? We are to seek first "His [Jesus'] righteousness"—the righteousness that He has given us—and all the things that we need will be added to us.

Beloved, when you know that your right standing with God always puts Him on your side, every fear will melt away like butter on a hot day. For if God is for you, who or what can successfully prevail against you?

"...I will gather the remnant of My flock out of all countries where I have driven them, and bring them back to their folds; and they shall be fruitful and increase. I will set up shepherds over them who will feed them; and they shall fear no more, nor be dismayed, nor shall they be lacking," says the Lord. "Behold, the days are coming," says the Lord, "That I will raise to David a Branch of righteousness; a King shall reign and prosper, and execute judgment and righteousness in the earth. In His days Judah will be saved, and Israel will dwell safely; now this is His name by which He will be called: THE LORD OUR RIGHTEOUSNESS."

—**JEREMIAH 23:3–6**

The Lord is my shepherd, I shall not be in want.

—**PSALM 23:1, NIV**

'The Lord Our Righteousness'

There's almost nothing more tender than the picture of a shepherd lovingly caring for his sheep.

Jeremiah 23:3–4 demonstrates a good shepherd's heart—to gather, protect and feed His sheep, so that they shall "be fruitful and increase". Jesus, our good shepherd, does all this through shepherds (pastors and teachers) He appoints over His people. Their role in representing Him is not to beat (shame) or fleece (financially exploit) the sheep, but to **feed** them such that they "shall fear no more, nor be dismayed, nor shall they be lacking".

Now, what is this "food" that brings the sheep to the place of no fear, no discouragement and no lack? It is "the Lord our Righteousness". Beloved, the more you feed on teaching that reveals Jesus and the gift of His righteousness through faith in His finished work, the more you'll experience freedom from fear, depression and lack. So pursue ministries that carry Jesus' heart for His sheep, that boldly proclaim *the Lord our Righteousness* and that reveal His abundance of grace—and experience His fruitfulness and increase!

The fruit of the righteous is a tree of life...

—PROVERBS 11:30

The name of the Lord is a strong tower; the righteous run to it and are safe.

—PROVERBS 18:10

...the righteous are bold as a lion.

—PROVERBS 28:1

Depend Solely On Jesus' Grace

A precious young lady who had been listening to my sermons wrote to me rejoicing over receiving a miracle that she had been believing God for. She shared:

This time, I didn't go to God with my good works and my obedience to try to earn this blessing. All I did was believe and confess how, through the finished work of Christ at the cross, I have the undeserved favor of God and His own righteousness. And even though I had failed the test and an interview, because of His favor, I still gained admission to a reputable university in Germany on a full scholarship. Depending on Jesus' grace alone, I received this breakthrough. I'm going to believe and confess His grace and love for me for the rest of my life!

Isn't it wonderful that when we depend on Jesus' grace alone, doors of opportunity, success and provision open to us? May this testimony encourage you in whatever you are believing God for today!

*For the promise that he would be the heir
of the world was not to Abraham or to his
seed through the law, but through
the righteousness of faith.*

—**ROMANS 4:13**

*And if you are Christ's, then you
are Abraham's seed, and heirs
according to the promise.*

—**GALATIANS 3:29**

The Promise Is Received By Faith

In Romans 4:13, it is clear that God's promise that Abraham and his seed would be heirs of the world was not through the law, but through the **righteousness of faith**.

Today, because we belong to Jesus, we are Abraham's seed and heirs according to the promise. And the more we believe that we are righteous in Christ, the more we will experience His provision. My friend, being an heir of the world and walking in Abraham's blessings of health, protection and abundant provision come by **faith**. This is believing that even though we don't deserve any blessing from God, we have been made righteous by the sacrifice and finished work of His Son, and qualify for all His blessings!

On the cross, Jesus took our sins and gave us His righteousness. He took our poverty and gave us His abundance. He took our shame and gave us His victory. Today, believe that you have been made righteous by Jesus' finished work and start walking in the blessings of Abraham!

＊

But the righteousness of faith speaks...
—**ROMANS 10:6**

And since we have the same spirit of faith, according to what is written, "I believed and therefore I spoke," we also believe and therefore speak.
—**2 CORINTHIANS 4:13**

Death and life are in the power of the tongue...
—**PROVERBS 18:21**

Sing, O barren, you who have not borne! Break forth into singing...
—**ISAIAH 54:1**

Speak Out Your Righteousness

Let me share something powerful with you about righteousness. In Romans 10:6, God's Word tells us that the "righteousness of faith speaks".

Now, what does this mean? It means that God encourages us to not just believe in our hearts that we are righteous, but to also speak it out!

So righteous one, declare your righteousness. Every day, boldly say, "Father, I thank You that I am righteous in Christ, not because of what I have done, but because of what Christ has done. It's a gift and I receive it with all my heart."

I believe that when you speak and declare your righteousness, good things happen. You become conscious of all the blessings and all the promises that are due the righteous. Instead of disqualifying yourself, you'll start to believe God for good success, favor and wisdom. Experiencing provision becomes effortless because you know your right standing in Christ. So stop disqualifying yourself and confess your righteousness!

The righteousness of faith
speaks.

So say, *"I am righteous in Christ!*

God's *favor, wisdom, provision* and *good success* are mine today!"

Thus says the Lord: "Cursed is the man who trusts in man and makes flesh his strength, whose heart departs from the Lord. For he shall be like a shrub in the desert, and shall not see when good comes, but shall inhabit the parched places in the wilderness, in a salt land which is not inhabited. Blessed is the man who trusts in the Lord, and whose hope is the Lord. For he shall be like a tree planted by the waters, which spreads out its roots by the river, and will not fear when heat comes; but its leaf will be green, and will not be anxious in the year of drought, nor will cease from yielding fruit.

—JEREMIAH 17:5–8

It is better to trust in the Lord than to put confidence in man. It is better to trust in the Lord than to put confidence in princes.

—PSALM 118:8–9

Be The Blessed Man Described In The Bible!

Who wouldn't want to be the blessed man in Jeremiah 17?

In both good and bad times, the blessed man thrives and reigns. He is like a tree planted by the waters, with its roots spread out by the river. When the heat is on—when the competition heats up or when there is a financial drought—he doesn't fear or worry. His "leaves" remain green— he stays young and fresh. And he continues to be fruitful—always succeeding and seeing the desired results, whether in his business, career, family life or ministry!

How do you enjoy the blessings of the blessed man? You look not to man but to **Jesus alone**. Looking to Jesus is to meditate on His Word, His unmerited favor and His gift of righteousness. Begin to truly put your trust and hope in Jesus, instead of in your own strength or other people. Then, get ready to thrive and be bountifully fruitful whether times are good or bad!

CHAPTER 4

How To Experience God's Provision

*Surely goodness and mercy shall follow me
all the days of my life...*
—**PSALM 23:6**

*And when he brings out his own sheep,
he goes before them; and the sheep
follow him...*
—**JOHN 10:4**

*I am the good shepherd. The good shepherd
gives His life for the sheep.*
—**JOHN 10:11**

*Oh, give thanks to the Lord, for He is good!
For His mercy endures forever.*
—**1 CHRONICLES 16:34**

Pursue The Good Shepherd

One day, when I was studying the Word, the Lord said to me, "Notice how goodness and mercy **follow** you in Psalm 23:6." Then, He brought me to John 10:4, where it describes how the shepherd goes before the sheep and **the sheep follow him**.

In a flash, the Lord opened my eyes to see a divine sequence: When you **follow or pursue Him**, the good shepherd, His goodness and mercy and all the blessings you need in life will follow after you!

My friend, don't pursue the blessings. Pursue Jesus, the blesser. As you pursue Him, you don't have to be concerned about the blessings because they will follow after you! In fact, the Hebrew translation of Psalm 23:6 is much stronger and more aggressive. It literally says, "Surely goodness and mercy shall HUNT ME DOWN all the days of my life!"

*You crown the year with Your goodness, and
Your paths drip with abundance.*

—PSALM 65:11

*My sheep hear My voice, and I know them,
and they follow Me.*

—JOHN 10:27

*But as it is written: "Eye has not seen, nor ear
heard, nor have entered into the heart of man
the things which God has prepared
for those who love Him."*

—1 CORINTHIANS 2:9

Tread Where Jesus Treads

Regardless of what experts say about the current economic situation, I have good news for you. As a child of God, your blessings this year are not dependent on the ebb and flow of the stock market.

You can expect good things to happen to you this year because God's Word declares it: "You crown the year with Your **goodness**, and Your paths drip with **abundance**"!

"Pastor Prince, God's Word says it, but how do I see it?"

Great question! The key to experiencing the blessings lies in Psalm 65:11 itself—"**Your paths** drip with abundance". In order to see His paths dripping with abundance, you would need to **follow** Him, wouldn't you? So to experience the Lord's goodness and abundance this year, keep listening to and beholding His grace and finished work. It's easy to follow His leading when you are tuned to His grace. And when you tread where He treads, you will run right into the blessings that He has already prepared for you!

You can't go wrong
when you
*FOLLOW
JESUS,*
the good shepherd.

*Be tuned to
His grace and*
**allow Him to
lead you**
*into the blessings He
has prepared for you!*

You crown the year with Your goodness, and Your paths drip with abundance.

—**PSALM 65:11**

…Listen carefully to Me, and eat what is good, and let your soul delight itself in abundance. Incline your ear, and come to Me. Hear, and your soul shall live…

—**ISAIAH 55:2–3**

So faith comes from hearing, and hearing by the word of Christ.

—**ROMANS 10:17, NASB**

Hear Your Way To God's Abundance

Because the Lord's pathways "drip" or overflow with abundance, following in His footsteps will cause you to walk in that abundance. And to follow Him, all you have to do is listen carefully to Him.

Look at Isaiah 55:2–3: "**Listen carefully** to Me, and eat what is *good*, and let your soul delight itself in *abundance*. **Incline your ear**, and come to Me. **Hear**, and your soul shall live".

So to eat what is good and delight your soul in abundance, *listen* to the Word of the Lord. If you desire to walk out of lack and walk into divine provision, *keep listening* to the preaching of the good news of Jesus' finished work. *Keep hearing* all that He has done for you to inherit all of God's goodness and abundance. Faith will come to deliver you out of chronic illnesses, fears, debt and depression, into divine health, wisdom, provision, fruitfulness and joy!

*If you will listen diligently to the voice of the Lord
your God…the Lord your God will set you high above
all the nations of the earth. And all these blessings shall
come upon you and overtake you if you heed the voice of
the Lord your God. Blessed shall you be in the city and
blessed shall you be in the field. Blessed shall be the fruit
of your body and the fruit of your ground and the fruit
of your beasts, the increase of your cattle and the young
of your flock. Blessed shall be your basket and your
kneading trough. Blessed shall you be when you come
in and blessed shall you be when you go out. The Lord
shall cause your enemies who rise up against you to be
defeated before your face; they shall come out against
you one way and flee before you seven ways.*

—**DEUTERONOMY 28:1–7, AMPC**

*For I am not ashamed of the gospel of Christ,
for it is the power of God to salvation for
everyone who believes…*

—**ROMANS 1:16**

Good Grades From Hearing The Good News

Let me share with you what hearing and hearing the good news of the gospel did for one student in my congregation.

This student had done badly in her mid-year examination, failing three core subjects. Her parents then started playing my messages in their home and car as often as they could. As this girl listened repeatedly to the messages, her parents shared with me that they noticed a dramatic change in her attitude toward her studies. She started to place her hope and reliance on God, and peace began to replace the stress of school.

Six months later, in her final-year examination, to her delight (and that of her parents), she scored really well in those core subjects and received two awards: one for being among the top students in class and another for having made the best progress! Whatever your challenge is today, continual listening to the gospel of Jesus leads to good success!

...the God of our Lord Jesus Christ, the Father of glory...give to you the spirit of wisdom and revelation in the knowledge of Him, the eyes of your understanding being enlightened; that you may know what is the hope of His calling, what are the riches of the glory of His inheritance in the saints, and what is the exceeding greatness of His power toward us who believe, according to the working of His mighty power.

—EPHESIANS 1:17–19

Your Answer Is Found In The Person Of Jesus

The solution to all your problems can be found in the person of Jesus.

My friend, if you are worried about your daily provisions, see Jesus as your *provider*—the One who multiplied five loaves and two small fish to feed more than 5,000 people with 12 baskets full of leftovers. If you need wisdom for a particular situation, see Jesus as your *wisdom*—the One who always has the right answer and response to every challenge. And know that He is *in* you and *with* you to guide you in your decision-making.

Beloved, ask the Holy Spirit to give you a *personal* revelation of Jesus in the area of your need. He Himself is *the* solution for your every need!

'*Holy Spirit,* open
my eyes to *see*
what I need to *see*
about *JESUS* for
my area of need.'

Set Free After A Revelation Of God's Love

A precious brother once wrote to me about how he had been depressed and defeated for many years because he saw God as an angry, unloving God—one whom he needed to please constantly.

It was only after Jesus had *revealed His finished work* to this man that he was set free from believing that he had to earn the Father's approval. This revelation of the Lord's perfect work on the cross also opened his eyes to see God's unconditional love for him, and freed him to experience healing and restoration in so many practical areas of his life.

Beloved, whatever your need is today, I encourage you to pray, "Holy Spirit, open my eyes to see Jesus as I need to today." When you have a revelation of Jesus that speaks to your area of need, you will find faith filling your heart to receive your miracle!

Grace and peace be multiplied to you in the knowledge of God and of Jesus our Lord, as His divine power has given to us all things that pertain to life and godliness, through the knowledge of Him who called us by glory and virtue.

—2 PETER 1:2–3

For I determined not to know anything among you except Jesus Christ and Him crucified.

—1 CORINTHIANS 2:2

Get To Know Your Savior More And More

The Bible says in 2 Peter 1:2, "Grace and peace be multiplied to you in the knowledge of God and of Jesus our Lord." In the original Greek, it actually says, "…through the knowledge of our God and Savior Jesus Christ."

So God's unmerited favor and His shalom-peace (health, provision and total well-being) are *multiplied* in your life through the knowledge of JESUS. The more you know Jesus, the more you will be able to tap into the ever-flowing supply of His favor, healing and provision!

Beloved, every answer you need, whether it has to do with your finances, health, career or family life, is found in knowing more about Jesus in a personal and intimate way. I pray that every day, as you study the Scriptures or listen to Christ-centered sermons, the Holy Spirit will open your eyes to see more of Jesus—His beauty, His love and grace toward you, and His finished work at Calvary!

*Love has been perfected among us in this: that
we may have boldness in the day of judgment;
because as He is, so are we in this world.*

—1 JOHN 4:17

*...let us run with endurance the race God has set
before us. We do this by keeping our eyes on Jesus,
the champion who initiates and
perfects our faith...*

—HEBREWS 12:1–2, NLT

Look At Jesus—His Reality Is Your Reality

When you look at yourself (your weaknesses) and your negative circumstances, it's easy to become seized with anxiety, fear and despair.

That's why God wants us to look away from ourselves and look at Jesus. In God's eyes, because He has placed us in Christ, Jesus' reality is our reality today—"as He is, **so are we** in this world"!

So don't focus on your vulnerability or the lack in your life and get discouraged. Ask yourself: Is Jesus abandoned, forgotten, sick and poor today? No, He is at the right hand of the Father, full of life, peace, joy and favor. All of heaven's resources are at His disposal. He is greatly blessed, highly favored and deeply loved by the Father today, and so are you!

To be Jesus-occupied like this is to see as God sees. And when you see as God sees, you will also see the grace and supply of the Lord swallow up every lack in your life!

*For You have made him [man] a little lower
than the angels, and You have crowned
[surrounded] him with glory and honor.*
—PSALM 8:5

*For the Lord God is our sun and our shield.
He gives us grace and glory.*
—PSALM 84:11, NLT

*And the glory which You gave Me I have
given them, that they may be one just
as We are one.*
—JOHN 17:22

See Yourself Crowned With Glory And Honor

As God's beloved child, redeemed and ransomed by Christ, not only are you surrounded by His favor, you are also crowned (surrounded) with *glory* and *honor*. I encourage you to see yourself encircled with the same glory and honor that Jesus has at the right hand of the Father today. What a picture to have of yourself!

My friend, instead of moaning about all the qualities you lack and feeling depressed, see yourself surrounded by glory and honor. For example, if you are looking for a job, preparing for an interview or hoping for a promotion, don't waste time worrying that others may be more capable or experienced than you. Instead, be conscious that there is an anointing on you because God's glory is upon you.

Believe that the next time you step into a room, that room will light up and the atmosphere will change for the better because you are crowned with His glory and honor!

*For the land which you go to possess is not like the land
of Egypt from which you have come, where you sowed
your seed and watered it by foot, as a vegetable garden;
but the land which you cross over to possess is a
land of hills and valleys, which drinks water
from the rain of heaven.*

—**DEUTERONOMY 11:10–11**

*…the Lord your God brings you into the land of which
He swore to your fathers, to Abraham, Isaac, and Jacob,
to give you large and beautiful cities which you did not
build, houses full of all good things, which you did not
fill, hewn-out wells which you did not dig, vineyards
and olive trees which you did not plant…*

—**DEUTERONOMY 6:10–11**

*…The Lord is my rock, my fortress and my deliverer; my
God is my rock, in whom I take refuge, my shield and
the horn of my salvation. He is my stronghold,
my refuge and my Savior…*

—**2 SAMUEL 22:2–3, NIV**

Look Up For Your Supply

When the Israelites were slaves in Egypt, they relied on the River Nile, a *natural* resource, for their supply of water. They depended entirely on their own hands to carry the water from the Nile and did not have to look to God at all for His supply. This is a picture of human self-effort.

On the other hand, in the promised land of Canaan that God had prepared for His beloved people, there was no River Nile to depend on. So they had to look up and **depend solely on the Lord** for the blessing of rain to fall upon their land.

Beloved, even as you labor diligently in your career today, what is your trust in? Is it in your self-efforts to provide for yourself, or is your dependence on the Lord to bless, increase and promote you? It's time to look up, especially in times of economic turmoil when the "Niles" of the world are drying up. Look up to Jesus for your supply!

Blessed is the man who walks not in the counsel of the ungodly...but his delight is in the law of the Lord, and in His law he meditates day and night. He shall be like a tree planted by the rivers of water, that brings forth its fruit in its season, whose leaf also shall not wither; and whatever he does shall prosper.

—PSALM 1:1–3

And the Word became flesh and dwelt among us, and we beheld His glory, the glory as of the only begotten of the Father, full of grace and truth.

—JOHN 1:14

but to those who are called, both Jews and Greeks, Christ the power of God and the wisdom of God.

—1 CORINTHIANS 1:24

Delight In Jesus Daily

The Bible tells us, "Blessed is the man who walks not in the counsel of the ungodly". This means that while there *is* wisdom in ungodly counsel, a blessed man does not depend on it nor walk in it. On the contrary, his delight is in the Word of God, which is the person of Jesus!

My friend, let your delight be in Jesus. See Him in every page of the Bible as you meditate on God's Word day and night.

Beloved, whose counsel are you walking in today for your provision? Be wary of ungodly counsel that promises you quick short-term gains that could cause you to get into a debt trap. Conversely, as you meditate on Jesus daily, you will enjoy the blessings of abundance as a by-product of just being in His presence! As you delight in Jesus, you will bring forth fruit in season, your leaf (your health) will not wither, and whatever you do becomes abundantly blessed!

*But of Him you are in Christ Jesus, who became
for us wisdom from God—and righteousness and
sanctification and redemption.*

—1 CORINTHIANS 1:30

*Wisdom is the principal thing; therefore
get wisdom. And in all your getting,
get understanding.*

—PROVERBS 4:7

*The Lord will guide you continually, and satisfy
your soul in drought...*

—ISAIAH 58:11

*If any of you lacks wisdom, let him ask of God,
who gives to all liberally and without reproach,
and it will be given to him.*

—JAMES 1:5

Wisdom Is The Principal Thing

The solution to money problems is the wisdom of God. Today, as you believe God for increase, I want to encourage you to ask God first for wisdom with regard to all the provision challenges that you are facing right now.

In the Book of James, we learn that if anyone lacks wisdom, "let him ask of God, who gives to all liberally and without reproach, and it will be given to him".

The wisdom of God will help you to identify and solve the money problems that you are currently experiencing. Don't prioritize accumulating material things. God's Word declares that wisdom is the **principal** thing. My friend, in all your getting, get wisdom and understanding!

*When wisdom enters your heart, and knowledge
is pleasant to your soul, discretion will preserve you;
understanding will keep you, to deliver you
from the way of evil...*
—**PROVERBS 2:10–12**

*I will instruct you and teach you in the way you
should go; I will counsel you and watch over you.*
—**PSALM 32:8, NIV**

Blessed is the man whom You instruct, O Lord...
—**PSALM 94:12**

*For whoever finds me [wisdom] finds life, and
obtains favor from the Lord.*
—**PROVERBS 8:35**

*Trust in the Lord with all your heart, and lean
not on your own understanding; in all your ways
acknowledge Him, and He shall direct your paths.*
—**PROVERBS 3:5–6**

Involve Jesus

You don't need a financial miracle when you are consistently walking in the wisdom of God. In other words, when you walk in His wisdom, you won't be surviving from one bailout to another, nor be in a constant state of financial crisis and lack.

My friend, God's provision of wisdom is abundant and I want to challenge you to tap into this powerful resource from heaven.

Before you make a career move, start a new business, or make a significant purchase or investment, involve Jesus. Don't exclude the Lord. When someone pressurizes you to sign an agreement because the offer is "only valid for today", take a step back. Don't make an emotional decision and rush into it. Wait upon the Lord. Be prepared to walk away from this "great opportunity" if you don't sense His peace and wisdom. Learning how to flow in divine wisdom will save you both precious time and money.

I returned and saw under the sun that—the race is not to the swift, nor the battle to the strong, nor bread to the wise, nor riches to men of understanding, nor favor to men of skill; but time and chance happen to them all.
—**ECCLESIASTES 9:11**

For You, O Lord, will bless the righteous; with favor You will surround him as with a shield.
—**PSALM 5:12**

For they [God's people] did not gain possession of the land by their own sword, nor did their own arm save them; but it was Your right hand, Your arm, and the light of Your countenance, because You favored them.
—**PSALM 44:3**

…in Your favor our horn is exalted.
—**PSALM 89:17**

The Race Is Not To The Swift

The world tells you that those with the qualifications, talents and experience get the jobs, promotions and high salaries.

My friend, though you live in this world, as God's beloved child, you need not be limited by it. You have God's favor—**His unmerited, unearned, undeserved grace**! Read Ecclesiastes 9:11—"The race is not to the swift, nor the battle to the strong..." So even if you are not the smartest, strongest, most knowledgeable or best looking in the natural, God can still give you good success **when you depend on His grace**.

Instead of mulling over your "disqualifications", be conscious of God's favor on you. Smile and say, "God's favor is all over me because of Jesus. I expect good things to happen to me today!" Beloved, be conscious of His favor. Believe it. Confess it. And you will experience it!

Take JESUS as your
WISDOM
and *make* all the
right decisions.

One moment of
GOD'S FAVOR
*can turn
your life around.*

May the favor of the Lord our God rest upon us; establish the work of our hands for us—yes, establish the work of our hands.

—**Psalm 90:17, niv**

But God has chosen the foolish things of the world to put to shame the wise, and God has chosen the weak things of the world to put to shame the things which are mighty; and the base things of the world and the things which are despised God has chosen, and the things which are not, to bring to nothing the things that are, that no flesh should glory in His presence.

—**1 Corinthians 1:27–29**

But while Joseph was there in the prison, the Lord was with him; He showed him kindness and granted him favor in the eyes of the prison warden.

—**Genesis 39:20–21, niv**

You have granted me life and favor, and Your care has preserved my spirit.

—**Job 10:12**

Have Big Dreams

Here's a story of a young man in my congregation who had started a small business distributing swimming pool equipment. When a massive tender for building the world's longest elevated swimming pool came up, this young man, who had been listening to my messages on depending on God's favor, decided to participate in the tender. Despite intense competition for this multi-million dollar construction project, this young man, who had never built a swimming pool in his life, was awarded the project!

He didn't have the qualifications or experience of his competitors, but he certainly had the favor of God. His first construction project became the world's most expensive swimming pool. It sits atop an iconic landmark in my country, suspended 57 storeys above the ground across three buildings, right in the heart of the city. Every time I drive past this landmark and look up to where this beautiful pool is, I am reminded of the goodness and favor of our Lord! Beloved, lean on God's favor and have big dreams!

So Ruth the Moabitess said to Naomi, "Please let me go to the field, and glean heads of grain after him in whose sight I may find favor." And she said to her, "Go, my daughter." Then she left, and went and gleaned in the field after the reapers. And she happened to come to the part of the field belonging to Boaz, who was of the family of Elimelech.

—**RUTH 2:2–3**

So she fell on her face, bowed down to the ground, and said to him [Boaz], "Why have I found favor in your eyes, that you should take notice of me, since I am a foreigner?"

—**RUTH 2:10**

Remember me, O Lord, with the favor You have toward Your people. Oh, visit me with Your salvation.

—**PSALM 106:4**

God's Provision Exceeds All Your Expectations

Are you believing God for a life partner? Trust the Lord to position you at the right place at the right time to meet the right person. Look at the story of Ruth. Of all the fields that she could have stepped into to collect grain, the Lord led her to Boaz's field! Boaz then fell in love with Ruth and the rest is history.

In the natural, all the odds were stacked against Ruth. She was a poor widow and a Moabitess (a foreigner). But that did not stop her from putting her trust in the Lord's favor. Now, that favor not only led to the provision of grain for her and her mother-in-law, Naomi, it also led to the provision of a blessed life partner.

Beloved, God's provision will exceed all your expectations! Ruth was only believing for grain, but the Lord exceeded her expectations and blessed her with Boaz! Believe with all your heart that Jesus can do the same for you!

*Then the Lord appeared to him and said:
"Do not go down to Egypt; live in the
land of which I shall tell you. Dwell in
this land, and I will be with you and bless
you; for to you and your descendants I
give all these lands, and I will perform
the oath which I swore to Abraham your
father."…So Isaac dwelt in Gerar.*

—**GENESIS 26:2–3, 6**

*Isaac planted crops in that land and the
same year reaped a hundredfold, because
the Lord blessed him.*

—**GENESIS 26:12, NIV**

Stay Put, Trust Jesus And Reap A Hundredfold!

Looking at the cracks that lined the parched earth, Isaac thought, "This famine is bad. Perhaps I should leave Gerar and go down to Egypt and plant my crops there." But when he looked up, the Lord appeared and said, "**Do not go down to Egypt**…Dwell in this land, and **I will be with you and bless you**…" So Isaac stayed put in Gerar.

When Isaac had stayed in Gerar for some time, he "planted crops in that land and the same year reaped a hundredfold, **because the Lord blessed him**". Do you see that? Despite the severe famine, Isaac's crops flourished and he had a most bountiful harvest! Beloved, stay put where God has called you—don't run to the world for help but keep depending on the Lord and His abounding favor. Don't give up on God. When your faith is in the One who multiplied the loaves and fish and who knows everything, you will flourish even in times of famine!

*Then Isaac sowed in that land, and reaped in the
same year a hundredfold; and the Lord blessed him.
The man began to prosper, and continued prospering
until he became very prosperous; for he had
possessions of flocks and possessions of herds
and a great number of servants.*

—**GENESIS 26:12–14**

*Arise, shine; for your light has come! And the glory of
the Lord is risen upon you. For behold, the darkness
shall cover the earth, and deep darkness the people;
but the Lord will arise over you, and His glory
will be seen upon you.*

—**ISAIAH 60:1–2**

Don't Fear The Famine—God Will Provide

Do you believe that you can experience the most increase when the world is experiencing famine?

My friend, famines have been around since the time of the Old Testament patriarchs. But the good news is that God always takes good care of His people. Abraham had more than enough *during a time of famine*. His son, Isaac, had enough to sow *during a time of famine* and reaped a hundredfold. In fact, Isaac began to experience the most abundant increase and provision during the time of famine.

That's God's style! All glory goes to Him when you and your loved ones are provided for during a famine. Beloved, fear not, but be confident and assured that Jesus will lead you into new levels of success and blessings. He will cause you to experience a hundredfold increase while the world is in famine.

When you keep your eyes on Jesus' abounding favor toward you...

...you don't have to be afraid in times of famine.

While the earth remains, seedtime and harvest,
cold and heat, winter and summer, and day
and night shall not cease.

—GENESIS 8:22

…He who sows sparingly will also reap sparingly, and
he who sows bountifully will also reap bountifully. So let
each one give as he purposes in his heart, not grudgingly
or of necessity; for God loves a cheerful giver. And God
is able to make all grace abound toward you, that you,
always having all sufficiency in all things, may have an
abundance for every good work…Now may He who
supplies seed to the sower, and bread for food, supply
and multiply the seed you have sown and increase the
fruits of your righteousness.

—2 CORINTHIANS 9:6–10

Give, and it will be given to you: good measure, pressed
down, shaken together, and running over will be put
into your bosom. For with the same measure that you
use, it will be measured back to you.

—LUKE 6:38

The Secret Of Sowing

The resources God blesses you with today contain both *bread* and *seed* for you. Don't consume all you have as bread. Have the wisdom to sow seeds that will provide you with *both* bread for the future *and* more seed to sow again.

The Bible tells us plainly that "he who sows sparingly will also reap sparingly, and he who sows bountifully will also reap bountifully", and encourages us to give purposefully, "not grudgingly or of necessity; for God loves a cheerful giver". Now, look at the provision promise that God gives when you sow bountifully: "God is able to make ALL GRACE ABOUND toward you, that you, always having all SUFFICIENCY in ALL things, may have an abundance for EVERY good work".

Beloved, the key to experiencing God's provision promise can be traced to how a person sows the seeds he receives. When your seed is sown, God will "multiply the seed you have sown and increase the fruits of your righteousness".

So he who had received five talents came and brought five other talents, saying, "Lord, you delivered to me five talents; look, I have gained five more talents besides them." His lord said to him, "Well done, good and faithful servant..." He also who had received two talents came and said, "Lord, you delivered to me two talents; look, I have gained two more talents besides them." His lord said to him, "Well done, good and faithful servant..."

—**MATTHEW 25:20–23**

He who has a slack hand becomes poor, but the hand of the diligent makes rich.

—**PROVERBS 10:4**

The sluggard craves and gets nothing, but the desires of the diligent are fully satisfied.

—**PROVERBS 13:4, NIV**

Give Jesus Something To Multiply

In the parable of the talents, the master commended the first two servants because they multiplied the money entrusted to them. They didn't laze around drinking tea, complaining about how hard it is to get a job in this economy. On the contrary, they were diligent, wise and prudent, and found ways to double the money that had been entrusted to them. The Lord then congratulated them and called them good and faithful servants.

My friend, I want to encourage you to be a diligent, wise, good and faithful steward of the money that God has placed in your hands. As you trust the Lord for His provision, spend money to send out your résumés, to go for interviews or even to upgrade yourself for a better job. Don't bury your money in the ground by sitting at home and watching television. Give Jesus something that He can multiply and you'll see Him put His favor upon it!

"Bring all the tithes into the storehouse, that there may be food in My house, and try Me now in this," says the Lord of hosts, "If I will not open for you the windows of heaven and pour out for you such blessing that there will not be room enough to receive it. And I will rebuke the devourer for your sakes, so that he will not destroy the fruit of your ground, nor shall the vine fail to bear fruit for you in the field," says the Lord of hosts; "And all nations will call you blessed, for you will be a delightful land," says the Lord of hosts.

—MALACHI 3:10–12

Honor the Lord with your possessions, and with the firstfruits of all your increase; so your barns will be filled with plenty, and your vats will overflow with new wine.

—PROVERBS 3:9–10

For if the firstfruit is holy, the lump is also holy; and if the root is holy, so are the branches.

—ROMANS 11:16

The Open Windows Of Heaven

Beloved, did you know that God doesn't need your tithe? And I tell my congregation not to tithe if they have no revelation of tithing. This is because nothing will happen if they tithe out of fear or religious obligation.

My friend, only tithe to your local church if you have a revelation that it is an act of worship and thanksgiving unto Jesus. You are saying, "Jesus, YOU are the source of all my blessings and increase. Thank You for always blessing me and my family out of the riches of Your grace."

When you tithe out of such a revelation, God declares, "I will…open for you the windows of heaven and pour out for you such blessing that there will not be room enough to receive it…I will rebuke the devourer for your sakes, so that he will not destroy the fruit of your ground, nor shall the vine fail to bear fruit for you in the field." Clearly, tithing is only for those of us who have a revelation of God's heart for our provision.

...he [Melchizedek] whose genealogy is not derived from them received tithes from Abraham and blessed him who had the promises. Now beyond all contradiction the lesser is blessed by the better. Here mortal men receive tithes, but there he receives them, of whom it is witnessed that he lives. Even Levi, who receives tithes, paid tithes through Abraham, so to speak, for he was still in the loins of his father when Melchizedek met him...For it is evident that our Lord arose from Judah, of which tribe Moses spoke nothing concerning priesthood. And it is yet far more evident if, in the likeness of Melchizedek, there arises another priest who has come, not according to the law of a fleshly commandment, but according to the power of an endless life. For He testifies: "You are a priest forever according to the order of Melchizedek."

—HEBREWS 7:6–10, 14–17

Your Tithe Testifies That Jesus Lives!

Today, when you tithe, Hebrews 7:8 tell us you are not tithing to mortal men, but to Christ who lives. You are tithing to Jesus our High Priest, whose priesthood is after the order of Melchizedek— according to the power of an *endless* life. That is why when you bring your tithes, you are declaring that Jesus is indeed alive in your life!

Do you know what it means to have Jesus alive in your life? It means that He will come into your negative circumstance and turn it around for your good! It means that there will be tokens, signs and wonders that He is alive in your life. People will look at you and say, "How is it you manage to stay so blessed despite the economic situation?"

Beloved, He will set you apart from the people of the world and provide abundantly for all your needs!

CHAPTER 5

*Rest Your Way Into
God's Provision*

"The Spirit of the Lord is upon Me, because He has anointed Me to preach the gospel to the poor; He has sent Me to heal the brokenhearted, to proclaim liberty to the captives and recovery of sight to the blind, to set at liberty those who are oppressed; to proclaim the acceptable year of the Lord."

—LUKE 4:18–19

Beloved, I pray that you may prosper in every way and [that your body] may keep well, even as [I know] your soul keeps well and prospers.

—3 JOHN 1:2, AMPC

Jesus Christ is the same yesterday, today, and forever.

—HEBREWS 13:8

Jesus' Heart Revealed

When Jesus was in a synagogue in Nazareth, He spoke of how God sent Elijah to the widow of Zarephath, and Elisha to Naaman the Syrian. If you read these two stories in the Old Testament, you will realize that one is a miracle of **provision and abundance** (the widow's last bit of oil was multiplied), while the other is a miracle of **healing** (Naaman was cleansed of leprosy).

So even in the Old Testament, we see that God's desire is to amply provide for and heal people. It's not His will for anyone to suffer lack, or to perish from disease. In the New Testament, when Jesus encountered lack, He gave huge catches of fish, and multiplied loaves and fish. When the sick came to Him, He always healed them.

Jesus is the same yesterday, today and forever. Settle it in your heart and mind that He wants you healthy and provided for. Take time to read all the miracles of provision and healing in the Gospels and see Jesus' heart for you today.

In Him we have redemption through His blood, the forgiveness of sins, according to the riches of His grace which He made to abound toward us in all wisdom and prudence.

—EPHESIANS 1:7–8

But God, who is rich in mercy, because of His great love with which He loved us, even when we were dead in trespasses, made us alive together with Christ (by grace you have been saved), and raised us up together, and made us sit together in the heavenly places in Christ Jesus, that in the ages to come He might show the exceeding riches of His grace in His kindness toward us in Christ Jesus.

—EPHESIANS 2:4–7

The Lord is merciful and gracious, slow to anger, and abounding in mercy.

—PSALM 103:8

Five-Minute Grace?

One reason many Christians fret and worry instead of turn to God when they face challenges is that they see His grace as limited. Just as they see their time as limited, their savings as limited and the earth's natural resources as limited, so they rationalize that God's grace must also be limited. How unfortunate it is when modern-day believers understand the word "grace" in terms of car parking charges—the five-minute "grace" period before the charges apply!

Beloved, when it comes to the Lord's grace, you must know that it is UNLIMITED! It's INFINITE! Who can fathom the depths of His immeasurable grace?

That's why God doesn't want you to take just a pinch of His grace once in a while and worry the rest of the time. No, He wants you to take an ABUNDANCE of it *every* single day for *every* single situation! Don't take just "five minutes" of grace. Take an abundance of it! That's how you live at rest and reign in life!

*For of His fullness we have all received,
and grace upon grace.*

—JOHN 1:16, NASB

*The faithful love of the Lord never ends! His
mercies never cease. Great is His faithfulness…*

—LAMENTATIONS 3:22–23, NLT

*If you then, being evil, know how to give good
gifts to your children, how much more will your
Father who is in heaven give good things to
those who ask Him!*

—MATTHEW 7:11

His Grace Never Ceases

Placing a handful of tokens onto the arcade game machine that my little Jessica was completely engrossed in, I said to her, "Jessica, once the game is ending, just put in another token, alright?" She was only three years old then, but certainly understood well enough how to keep on inserting new tokens to keep the game going.

It was fun watching her enjoy the game. Her eyes would light up and her dimples would show, especially when she was winning. As her father, seeing her happy always makes me happy, so I kept watch to ensure that she had sufficient tokens to keep the game going. Once they ran low, I would rush to the counter to get a new stack of tokens. So Jessica's daddy kept supplying more tokens while she simply kept enjoying the game.

Beloved, if an earthly father can do this for his daughter for a simple arcade game, how **much more** will our heavenly Father, who loves us and delights in seeing us blessed, do to provide for us!

But Noah found grace in the eyes of the Lord.
—GENESIS 6:8

*Come to Me, all you who labor and are heavy
laden, and I will give you rest.*
—MATTHEW 11:28

So let us do our best to enter that rest...
—HEBREWS 4:11, NLT

Rest Finds Grace

When a subject is mentioned for the first time in the Bible, there is usually an important truth we can learn. So do you know when or where the word "grace" is first mentioned in the Bible? It's in Genesis 6:8—"But Noah found **grace** in the eyes of the Lord".

"So what's the important truth to be learned here, Pastor Prince?"

My friend, the name "Noah" means "rest". Therefore, the powerful truth here is that REST FINDS GRACE! The more you **rest** in the finished work of Jesus, and do what you need to do out of that rest, the more His grace will operate in your life and cause you to experience His blessings! When you go about your work, studies or household chores resting in the knowledge that the Lord's favor is on you and blessing the work of your hands, you can't help but see His supernatural results and provision.

Beloved, learn to rest and find grace in the eyes of the Lord!

LET GO and REST

in His love for you.

Rest—The Most Responsible Thing You Can Do

If I don't worry about my kids and their studies, I'm not being a responsible mother. If I don't work overtime seven days a week to make more money for my family, I'm not being a good father.

My friend, the desires you have to provide for your family are valid. But by worrying and being stressed out, not only do you harm your health and relationships, but you also constrict the supply of God's grace in your life. God cannot work freely in your life when you are "in the way", worrying and getting stressed as you do things out of fear.

Beloved, the most responsible thing you can do for yourself and your family is to **let go and rest**! REST in His love and favor toward you and your family. Step aside and let **Jesus** do for you what you cannot do for yourself. And when you let Him do it, not only will there be more results, but you will also experience peace and good success!

*So she [Ruth] gleaned in the field until evening,
and beat out what she had gleaned, and it was
about an ephah of barley.*

—**RUTH 2:17**

*So she [Ruth] lay at his [Boaz's] feet until
morning, and she arose before one could
recognize another. Then he said, "Do not let it
be known that the woman came to the threshing
floor." Also he said, "Bring the shawl that is
on you and hold it." And when she held it, he
measured six ephahs of barley, and laid it on
her. Then she went into the city.*

—**RUTH 3:14–15**

Rest Brings Far More Results

When Ruth worked from morning to evening in the field of Boaz, a wealthy relative, she collected only **one** ephah of barley. That's about 10 days' supply. But when she simply rested overnight at his feet, he gave her **six** ephahs of barley—about two months' supply!

Boaz, Ruth's kinsman redeemer, is a picture of Jesus our Redeemer, whom we are to rest in. This rest refers to an inner posture of trust and quiet confidence in Jesus' finished work and in His ability to give you increase and good success *as you go about doing what you need to do*. Rest is not sitting around, doing nothing and waiting for His blessings to fall into our laps.

Beloved, what God doesn't want you to do is worry and do things out of fear. He wants you to rest at Jesus' feet and listen to His words of love and life. Let Him drive out your fears and lead you to good success!

*Now don't worry about a thing, my daughter
[Ruth]. I [Boaz] will do what is necessary…while
it's true that I am one of your family redeemers,
there is another man who is more closely related
to you than I am…in the morning I will talk to
him. If he is willing to redeem you, very well. Let
him marry you. But if he is not willing, then as
surely as the Lord lives, I will redeem
you myself…*

—RUTH 3:11–13, NLT

*Then she [Naomi] said, "Sit still, my daughter,
until you [Ruth] know how the matter will turn
out; for the man [Boaz] will not rest until he has
concluded the matter this day."*

—RUTH 3:18

When You Rest, God Works

Boaz wanted to redeem Ruth from all her financial woes and marry her. However, according to the custom of the day, he could do so only after a relative closer to Ruth gave up his right to redeem Ruth. So Boaz went to the gate of Bethlehem to settle the matter with this relative.

When Ruth's mother-in-law, Naomi, heard what had transpired, she told Ruth to **sit still and not be anxious**, because Boaz **would not rest** until he had successfully resolved the matter concerning Ruth that very day. Now, because Boaz is a picture of Jesus, our kinsman Redeemer, the truth here is that when we "sit still" and not be anxious, Jesus goes to work on our behalf!

Beloved, what provision challenge are you facing today? A troubling bodily symptom? The fear of losing your job? Commit the matter to your heavenly Boaz, Jesus, and **rest** in His ability, His willingness and His favor. When you rest in Him, He will not rest until He has successfully resolved the matter for you!

Let us labor therefore to enter into that rest...

—**Hebrews 4:11, KJV**

And on the seventh day God ended His work which He had done, and He rested on the seventh day from all His work which He had done. Then God blessed the seventh day and sanctified it, because in it He rested from all His work which God had created and made.

—**Genesis 2:2–3**

Unless the Lord builds the house, they labor in vain who build it; unless the Lord guards the city, the watchman stays awake in vain. It is vain for you to rise up early, to sit up late, to eat the bread of sorrows; for so He gives His beloved sleep.

—**Psalm 127:1–2**

Work At Resting

There are so many things to do every day—prepare breakfast, drive the kids to school, finish up your presentation, chair a meeting, meet a client, counsel a friend…It's like we're always working on something!

Actually, if there's one thing we ought to prioritize working on every day, it is working at being at **rest**! Sounds like an oxymoron, doesn't it? How can you *work* at *resting*?

Yet, that is exactly what God wants us to do. Given our inclination to work, worry and rush to finish all our tasks every day, He wants us to prioritize spending time with Him, and letting His love and words of grace flush out all our agitations, worries and fears.

My friend, make laboring to enter God's rest *number one* on your to-do list every day. When you are at rest, God's grace can flow unhindered through you to accomplish—with ease—all that needs to be accomplished for the day. Rest is His provision for you today—receive it!

Rest is not
inactivity but
God-directed
activity.

What Rest Means And How It Works

Some believers have peculiar notions about what rest really means. They think that rest means that they are not to do anything but wait for God's provision to magically appear before them.

But biblical rest is not inactivity. It is directed activity! God blesses us as we trust Him and step out in faith. For example, if you're looking for a life partner, don't stay home waiting for that special someone. A complete stranger is not going to show up at your door with a marriage proposal. But as you rest in God's favor, and as you make yourself available to meet the right kind of people (for example, by getting involved in a ministry in church), the Holy Spirit will direct your steps and cause your path to cross with your future life partner's.

Beloved, it is the same for every provision you are looking to Christ for. He has already accomplished all for you to receive God's best, so rest in His favor and unfailing love for you. Then, as you step out in faith, you'll see Him bless you beyond your wildest dreams!

*Which of you by worrying can add one cubit
to his stature?*

—**MATTHEW 6:27**

*And Jesus increased in wisdom and stature, and
in favor with God and men.*

—**LUKE 2:52**

*And the child Samuel grew in stature, and in favor
both with the Lord and men.*

—**1 SAMUEL 2:26**

Grace For Parenting

If you are overwhelmed by the responsibilities of being a parent today, I want to encourage you to believe that there is a provision and a grace for parenting. Instead of worrying and being anxious for your children, pray for them to experience God's wisdom, favor and protection through Jesus Christ.

Before they go to bed at night, or before they leave for school, just lay hands on them and say, "Because you are a Jesus-boy (or Jesus-girl), day by day, you are increasing **in the wisdom of God and in favor with God and men**! Jesus will cause you to be at the right place at the right time."

Cast your cares for your children to the Lord. Trust Him for the provision of wisdom to speak words of encouragement and life to them about making good decisions instead of bowing to peer pressure. The Lord has equipped and provided you with the grace to be an excellent parent!

For with stammering lips and another tongue He will speak to this people, to whom He said, "This is the rest with which You may cause the weary to rest," and, "This is the refreshing"...

—ISAIAH 28:11–12

He who speaks in a tongue edifies himself...

—1 CORINTHIANS 14:4

And the Holy Spirit helps us in our weakness. For example, we don't know what God wants us to pray for. But the Holy Spirit prays for us with groanings that cannot be expressed in words. And the Father who knows all hearts knows what the Spirit is saying, for the Spirit pleads for us believers in harmony with God's own will.

—ROMANS 8:26–27, NLT

Tongues—The Rest And The Refreshing

The prophet Isaiah describes speaking in tongues as "the rest" and "the refreshing". In the New Testament, the apostle Paul tells us that the believer who speaks in a tongue "edifies himself". The word "edify" here is *oikodomeo*, which means to *build up, restore* and *repair*.

I have found all this to be true, especially when I'm tired after a long flight. Many a time, despite the jet lag, praying in the Holy Spirit has given me a supernatural rest and energy to carry on preaching and ministering!

My friend, one of the best ways to be refreshed, to enter into rest and remain restful is to pray in tongues throughout the day. You can pray in tongues under your breath on your way to work or while having your coffee break. If you are a homemaker, you can pray in tongues while cooking or doing the laundry. Beloved, when you involve the **Holy Spirit** and are **restful**, how can you not experience His supernatural provision in everything you do?

When the Spirit of truth comes, He will guide you into all truth. He will not speak on His own but will tell you what He has heard. He will tell you about the future.

—JOHN 16:13, NLT

For all who are led by the Spirit of God are children of God.

ROMANS 8:14, NLT

And we know that God causes everything to work together for the good of those who love God and are called according to His purpose for them.

—ROMANS 8:28, NLT

Rest Is Holy Spirit-Directed Activity

One of the great benefits of praying in tongues is that it sensitizes you to the leading of the Holy Spirit. A brother from our church was tormented by panic attacks and depressed to the point of being suicidal. He had other health issues too and had to take many pills each night just to get a bit of sleep.

But he started to pray in tongues after he heard me preach on the subject, and experienced divine peace. Every day, he just prayed in tongues. The more he did that, the more he was tuned to the Spirit's leading in the areas of his diet, medication and health. Led by the Spirit, he finally got out of his nine-year ordeal!

My friend, rest is not inactivity or laziness, but **Holy Spirit-directed activity**. The more you pray in tongues, the more you'll sense the Spirit's leading. He will lead you out of your valley of depression, debt or disease, and bring you to a high place of health and wholeness!

...the Lord Jesus on the same night in which He was betrayed took bread; and when He had given thanks, He broke it and said, "Take, eat; this is My body which is broken for you; do this in remembrance of Me."

—1 Corinthians 11:23–24

Then He took the cup, and gave thanks, and gave it to them, saying, "Drink from it, all of you. For this is My blood of the new covenant, which is shed for many for the remission of sins."

—Matthew 26:27–28

So when Jesus had received the sour wine, He said, "It is finished!" And bowing His head, He gave up His spirit.

—John 19:30

Daily Communion With The Lord

Why do we take the Holy Communion? Is it to get something out of the Lord? No, taking the Communion reminds us of what Jesus has **already** provided and accomplished for us at the cross.

My friend, has Jesus already made provision for our sins at the cross? Yes! Then you no longer have to live feeling condemned for your sins. Has Jesus already made provision for our healing at the cross? Yes! Then you no longer have to accept the disease in your body, and you can start believing Jesus for total healing. Has Jesus already made provision for our lack on the cross? Yes! Then you no longer have to accept lack and can start believing Jesus for His abundance to start flowing and manifesting in your life.

Beloved, take the Communion daily and have a fresh revelation of all the good that Jesus has already made provision for through His finished work.

But He was wounded for our transgressions, He was bruised for our iniquities; the chastisement for our peace was upon Him, and by His stripes we are healed.

—**Isaiah 53:5**

...Himself bore our sins in His own body on the tree, that we, having died to sins, might live for righteousness—by whose stripes you were healed.

—**1 Peter 2:24**

Family Healed Of Food Allergies

A lady from the United Kingdom wrote in to share how taking the Holy Communion and **seeing Jesus' finished work** have delivered her and her family from gluten and dairy food intolerance:

*None of us could eat dairy foods or foods containing gluten. Our diet was very restricted... However, when we heard the messages on the Holy Communion and the perfect exchange Jesus performed on the cross, we decided that it had to be the truth, and therefore we **were already healed**.*

*We took the Holy Communion, declaring that by Jesus' stripes we **had been healed** and from that day on we have been eating normally...For over a year now, we have been completely well and able to try so many new foods!*

Beloved, the work is finished. Whenever you hold the bread and cup in your hands believing this, you will receive Jesus' provision of health for your body!

You prepare a table before me in the presence of my enemies; You anoint my head with oil; my cup runs over. Surely goodness and mercy shall follow me all the days of my life; and I will dwell in the house of the Lord forever.

—**Psalm 23:5–6**

Let God arise, let His enemies be scattered...

—**Psalm 68:1**

The Lord will cause your enemies who rise against you to be defeated before your face; they shall come out against you one way and flee before you seven ways.

—**Deuteronomy 28:7**

A Table In The Presence Of Your Enemies

Heartbroken and devastated when her 18-year-old daughter told her that she hated her and left home, a mother from Texas developed high blood pressure and started hemorrhaging badly.

One day, she tuned in to one of my broadcasts and heard me preach about Jesus' finished work at Calvary. She got my series on the Holy Communion and took it every day as she looked to the Lord's finished work to heal her body and restore her relationship with her daughter.

Six months later, this same mother wrote to tell me that she was healed of high blood pressure and no longer bleeding. God was also restoring her relationship with her daughter who had returned home. Today, she is taking Communion daily with her husband and children, and experiencing the blessed family life she had once only dreamed of. Beloved, no matter how bad things may be now, rest in Jesus' finished work by coming to the Lord's table, and receive your victory, restoration and wholeness!

Surely He has borne our griefs (sicknesses, weaknesses, and distresses) and carried our sorrows and pains [of punishment], yet we [ignorantly] considered Him stricken, smitten, and afflicted by God [as if with leprosy]. But He was wounded for our transgressions, He was bruised for our guilt and iniquities; the chastisement [needful to obtain] peace and well-being for us was upon Him, and with the stripes [that wounded] Him we are healed and made whole.

—ISAIAH 53:4–5, AMPC

For you are becoming progressively acquainted with and recognizing more strongly and clearly the grace of our Lord Jesus Christ (His kindness, His gracious generosity, His undeserved favor and spiritual blessing), [in] that though He was [so very] rich, yet for your sakes He became [so very] poor, in order that by His poverty you might become enriched (abundantly supplied).

—2 CORINTHIANS 8:9, AMPC

Crushed For Our Total Well-Being

How is holy anointing oil produced? By crushing olives in an oil press to extract the oil. This is a beautiful picture of the crushing of our Lord Jesus, which began in the Garden of Gethsemane. "Gethsemane" literally means "oil press".

The Bible tells us that He was *pierced* for our transgressions. He was *crushed* for our iniquities. The *punishment* that brought us peace was upon Him, and by His *stripes* we are healed.

Jesus came to be crushed for us. He came to be bruised, scourged and pierced. Why? So that all that He is—health, life, wholeness, abundance, fruitfulness, grace, goodness—can flow out like golden oil into our lives!

My friend, whenever you use the holy anointing oil for healing, provision or protection, remember that Jesus has already been crushed for your total well-being. See the work as completely finished and enter into rest. That's how you receive your victory!

Is anyone among you sick? Let him call for the elders of the church, and let them pray over him, anointing him with oil in the name of the Lord. And the prayer of faith will save the sick, and the Lord will raise him up. And if he has committed sins, he will be forgiven.

—JAMES 5:14–15

It shall come to pass in that day that his burden will be taken away from your shoulder, and his yoke from your neck, and the yoke will be destroyed because of the anointing oil.

—ISAIAH 10:27

He personally bore our sins in His [own] body on the tree [as on an altar and offered Himself on it]…By His wounds you have been healed.

—1 PETER 2:24, AMPC

…by His stripes we are healed.

—ISAIAH 53:5

Health Through The Oil, Bread And Wine

A brother from New Zealand shared an amazing healing testimony with me. After undergoing two surgeries, he was diagnosed with grade eight prostate cancer and given a grim report by his specialist.

A couple, who were elders from his church, anointed him with oil and prayed over him. He felt God's power go through him. Following this, his wife would anoint him every night with a bottle of oil, and they would pray and take the Holy Communion together. His symptoms started to disappear and he began to feel so much better.

At his next checkup, his specialist was amazed. She proclaimed his blood test report "fantastic" because it showed all indicators in the normal range!

Beloved, the oil, bread and wine represent Jesus' finished work at the cross. Jesus provided His own body to be punished for the healing of your diseases and afflictions. Rest in the reality that by His stripes you are healed!

looking unto Jesus, the author and finisher of our faith, who for the joy that was set before Him endured the cross, despising the shame, and has sat down at the right hand of the throne of God.

—HEBREWS 12:2

I have been crucified with Christ; it is no longer I who live, but Christ lives in me; and the life which I now live in the flesh I live by faith in the Son of God, who loved me and gave Himself for me.

—GALATIANS 2:20

"...all things are possible to him who believes."

—MARK 9:23

Rest In Jesus Whose Faith Never Wavers

Did you know that our faith can sometimes stand in the way of us receiving our miracles? How? When our faith is in our faith and we are preoccupied with it. Instead of looking unto Jesus, we look at ourselves and ask, "Do I have enough faith?" or "Did I pray with enough faith?"

My friend, it's not about faith in your faith, but faith in the person of JESUS, whose faith is perfect and never wavers! When you are preoccupied with Jesus—His goodness, grace and compassion toward you—you will have unconscious faith. When you see His grace, God sees your faith!

Beloved, stop trying to muster up more faith. Simply rest in Christ who has all the faith for your miracle. Jesus has no doubt that His finished work is enough to bring about your breakthrough. All you need to do is see His grace and latch onto His faith that never wavers, and receive the provision and breakthrough you need!

Jesus is the
only one whose faith
never wavers.

Latch onto *His unwavering faith* and *receive* your provision.

"*Are you tired? Worn out? Burned out on religion? Come to Me. Get away with Me and you'll recover your life. I'll show you how to take a real rest. Walk with Me and work with Me—watch how I do it. Learn the unforced rhythms of grace. I won't lay anything heavy or ill-fitting on you. Keep company with Me and you'll learn to live freely and lightly.*"

—*MATTHEW 11:28–30, THE MESSAGE*

Jesus Gives You True Rest

Jesus lived in the unforced rhythms of grace. Everything He said and did was beautiful, perfectly timed. Always at the right place at the right time doing the right thing, His every word and deed went up to the Father as a sweet-smelling aroma.

My friend, Jesus wants you to learn His unforced rhythms of grace. He wants you to flow with Him. He's not hard to follow—His yoke is not heavy or burdensome. It is easy and light. When you walk in His ways, you will find true rest.

Beloved, Jesus' ways are not rash and impatient. He will never give you a prompting to spend more than you have. He will never lead you into a place of lack. Instead, He will lead you to see God's goodness that is already evident in your life. He will lead you to faithfully and diligently step from one level of increase to another. As you keep company with Him, He will teach you how to live the Christ-life.

The Lord has appeared of old to me, saying:
"Yes, I have loved you with an everlasting love;
therefore with lovingkindness I have
drawn you."

—**JEREMIAH 31:3**

As the Father loved Me, I also have loved you;
abide in My love.

—**JOHN 15:9**

For I am persuaded that neither death nor life,
nor angels nor principalities nor powers, nor
things present nor things to come, nor height
nor depth, nor any other created thing, shall be
able to separate us from the love of God which
is in Christ Jesus our Lord.

—**ROMANS 8:38–39**

You Are The Disciple Whom Jesus Loves

I used to think that of all the disciples Jesus loved, John was most loved by the Lord because the Bible calls him "the disciple whom Jesus loved". Then one day, I discovered that the phrase "the disciple whom Jesus loved" only appears in John's own Gospel. In other words, it was John who called himself the disciple whom Jesus loved!

Was John being arrogant? Did Jesus love him more than the rest? No, Jesus loved all 12 disciples the same, but John personalized and practiced Jesus' love for him!

My friend, that's what you ought to do too. Don't just say, "Yes, yes, Jesus loves *everybody*." Say, "Jesus loves ME!" Say, "I am the student whom Jesus loves," or "I am the disciple whom Jesus loves," or "I am the mom whom Jesus loves!" Every day, personalize, practice and rest in Jesus' love for you. Expect good things to happen to you when you believe that Jesus loves YOU in an intimate and personal way!

... *"You are My beloved Son, in whom
I am well pleased."*
—**MARK 1:11**

*to the praise of the glory of His grace, by which
He made us accepted in the Beloved.*
—**EPHESIANS 1:6**

*Then David put his hand in his bag and took
out a stone; and he slung it and struck the
Philistine in his forehead, so that the stone
sank into his forehead, and he fell on his face
to the earth. So David prevailed over the
Philistine with a sling and a stone, and
struck the Philistine and killed him...*
—**1 SAMUEL 17:49–50**

Know You Are God's Beloved And Win

As Jesus came out of the waters of baptism, the heavens parted, the Spirit descended upon Him, and the Father said to Him, "You are My beloved Son, in whom I am well pleased." Then, going into the wilderness in the power of knowing that He was the Father's beloved, our Lord Jesus overcame every one of the devil's temptations.

My friend, when you know that you *are* the Father's beloved because you are in Christ the Beloved, you will have the power to overcome every challenge the devil throws at you. Now, you are probably familiar with the story of David and Goliath. But did you know that David's name means "beloved"? It takes one who knows that he is God's beloved to bring down the giants in life!

So whether your giant is a financial crisis, chronic illness or destructive addiction, rest in the knowledge that you are God's beloved. It will strengthen and sustain you, and give you the faith, favor and wisdom to knock your giants down!

Good things happen
to *you* when
you **believe** that
*Jesus loves
you.*

YOU are God's
beloved,
in whom He is
well pleased.

*And we have known and believed the love that
God has for us. God is love, and he who abides
in love abides in God, and God in him.*

—1 JOHN 4:16

*How precious is Your steadfast love, O God!
The children of men take refuge and put their
trust under the shadow of Your wings.*

—PSALM 36:7, AMPC

*Now this is the confidence that we have in
Him, that if we ask anything according to His
will, He hears us. And if we know that He
hears us, whatever we ask, we know that we
have the petitions that we have asked of Him.*

—1 JOHN 5:14–15

Blessings Of The Lord's Beloved

Jesus loves ME. Three simple words that can make a big difference in your life when you believe them.

For some time, a precious lady in the Netherlands had been believing God for a financial provision. Then, she watched one of my television broadcasts and caught a revelation of how much the Lord loves her. For the first time, she prayed for her financial need with the revelation that Jesus loves her. "That very day," she said, "two new clients called me. The following week, I asked God again for His provision, simply trusting and resting in His love for me. Guess what? Three new clients called! Now, I know it is because Jesus loves me that He blesses me. It's not because of what I've done or not done. Getting a revelation of this truth has made such a difference that I am sharing it with my family, relatives and every person I meet!"

Breakthroughs come and amazing things can begin to happen to you when you truly believe how much Jesus loves YOU.

And Jesus said to him, "Foxes have holes and birds of the air have nests, but the Son of Man has nowhere to lay His head."

—MATTHEW 8:20

So when Jesus had received the sour wine, He said, "It is finished!" And bowing His head, He gave up His spirit.

—JOHN 19:30

Who shall separate us from the love of Christ? Shall tribulation, or distress, or persecution, or famine, or nakedness, or peril, or sword?…Yet in all these things we are more than conquerors through Him who loved us.

—ROMANS 8:35-37

More Than Conquerors Through Jesus' Love

Jesus said, "Foxes have holes and birds of the air have nests, but the Son of Man has nowhere to **lay** His head." I find this statement so beautiful. Let me tell you why.

In the original Greek text, the word for "lay" is a very unique word, *klino*. The only other place it is used in terms of Jesus resting His head is at the cross. When Jesus hung on the cross and cried, "It is finished!" the Bible says, "And **bowing** His head, He gave up His spirit." The word "bowing" here is the same Greek word, *klino*.

Beloved, it was only at the cross that the Son of Man finally found a place to rest His head. Jesus found His *rest* in redeeming us, in **loving us**. We, in turn, find *rest* in feeding on His sacrificial love for us. Whatever the challenge or need you are facing today, He has made you more than a conqueror through His love!

For all the promises of God in Him are Yes, and in Him Amen, to the glory of God through us.
—**2 Corinthians 1:20**

As each one has received a gift, minister it to one another, as good stewards of the manifold grace of God.
—**1 Peter 4:10**

The Lord will open to you His good treasure, the heavens, to give the rain to your land in its season, and to bless all the work of your hand. You shall lend to many nations, but you shall not borrow. And the Lord will make you the head and not the tail; you shall be above only, and not be beneath…
—**Deuteronomy 28:12–13**

"For I know the plans I have for you," declares the Lord, "plans to prosper you and not to harm you, plans to give you hope and a future."
—**Jeremiah 29:11, NIV**

Arise And Shine!

Beloved, all of God's provision promises toward you are *yes* and *Amen*! Right now, I want you to say these words out loud:

I declare that I am special in Jesus' eyes, and He loves me unconditionally. I have an awesome destiny. Jesus has equipped me with gifts, talents and abilities. Today, I receive the abundance of grace and the gift of righteousness to reign in life. I give thanks that His favor surrounds me like a shield and opens doors of opportunities for me. Because of Jesus, I shall be the head and not the tail, above and not beneath, the lender and not the borrower. I shall not suffer lack but be surrounded by His abundance, His wisdom, His peace and His protection.

Thank You, Jesus, for Your finished work at the cross for me. I receive a fresh revelation of Your love right now and thank You that everything my hands touch shall be blessed! I believe with all my heart that I am greatly blessed, highly favored and deeply loved! Amen!

Prayers

Salvation Prayer

If you would like to receive all that Jesus has done for you and make Him your Lord and Savior, please pray this prayer:

Lord Jesus, thank You for loving me and dying for me on the cross. Your precious blood washes me clean of every sin. You are my Lord and Savior, now and forever. I believe that You rose from the dead and that You are alive today. Because of Your finished work, I am now a beloved child of God and heaven is my home. Thank You for giving me eternal life and filling my heart with Your peace and joy. Amen.

Holy Communion Prayer

As you partake of the Holy Communion, keep seeing and declaring how you have been healed by Jesus' stripes. Keep seeing and declaring how His blood has washed away all your sins and qualified you to receive all of God's blessings, including His righteousness, provision and restoration.

Hold the bread in your hand and say this:

Thank You, Jesus, for Your broken body. Thank You for bearing my symptoms and sicknesses at the cross so that I may have Your health and wholeness. I declare that by Your stripes, by the beatings You bore, by the lashes which fell on Your back, I am completely healed. I believe and I receive Your resurrection life in my body today. (Eat the bread.)

Next, take the cup in your hand and say this:

Thank You, Jesus, for Your blood that has washed me whiter than snow. Your blood has brought me forgiveness and made me righteous forever. And as I drink, I celebrate and partake of the inheritance of the righteous, which includes provision, restoration and wholeness in every area of my life. (Drink the wine.)

Thank You, Jesus. I love You because You first loved me.

Anointing Oil Prayer

You may approach a pastor or leader in church to pray over and consecrate your oil for you. As a king and priest in Christ (Revelation 1:6), you can also pray over the oil and set it apart to be holy. Here's a prayer for blessing and sanctifying your oil:

In the name of Jesus, I set this oil apart to be holy anointing oil.

Jesus, I thank You that You were crushed for my complete healing and wholeness. This holy anointing oil speaks of the perfection of Your finished work. I thank You that whatever this oil touches, the fullness of Your grace, power, provision and healing virtue will flow, according to Your Word in Mark 6:13, James 5:14 and Isaiah 10:27.

I pray that wherever this oil is applied, it will bring glory and praise to Your name. Amen.

Medical Disclaimer

If you are facing a physical or mental health condition, please understand that this book is not meant to take the place of professional medical advice. If you or your loved one has a health concern or an existing medical condition, please do consult a qualified medical practitioner or healthcare provider. We would also advise you to ask and seek the Lord always for His wisdom and guidance regarding your specific health or medical issue, and to exercise godly wisdom in the management of your own physical, mental, and emotional well-being. Do not, on your own accord, disregard any professional medical advice or diagnosis. Please also do not take what has been shared in this book as permission or encouragement to stop taking your medication or going for medical treatment. While we make no guarantees and recognize that different individuals experience different results, we continue to stand in faith to believe and affirm God's Word and healing promises with all who believe.

We Would Like To Hear From You

If you have prayed the salvation prayer, or if you have a testimony to share after reading this book, please tell us about it via JosephPrince.com/testimony.